Diary of a Guerrilla

Ramón "Tianguis" Pérez

Translated by Dick J. Reavis

Arte Público Press
Houston, Texas
1999

Recovering the past, creating the future

Arte Público Press
University of Houston
Houston, Texas 77204-2174

Cover design by James F. Brisson

Pérez, Ramón (Tianguis)
  [Diario de un guerrilla. English]
  Diary of a guerrilla / by Ramón "Tianguis" Pérez.
  p.   cm.
  ISBN 1-55885-282-4 (clothbound)
  1. Pérez, Ramón (Tianguis) — Youth. 2. Zapotec Indians —
Biography. 3. Guerillas — Mexico — Biography. 4. Zapotec Indians
— Wars. 5. Zapotec Indians — Land tenure. 6. Peasantry — Mexico
— History — 20th century. 7. Peasant uprisings — Mexico —
History — 20th century. I. Title.
F1221.Z3P44   1999
972'.740832'092—dc21   99-24884
[B]   CIP

♾ The paper used in this publication meets the requirements of the American
National Standard for Information Sciences—Permanence of Paper for Printed
Library Materials, ANSI Z39.48-1984.

9 0 1 2 3 4 5 6 7 8   10 9 8 7 6 5 4 3 2 1

Translator's Foreword

Today's headlines from Mexico are often about the actions and pronouncements of guerrillas. The Zapatista movement in Chiapas and its spokesman, Subcomandante Marcos, are known around the globe. Less heralded but subject to increasing mention is the shadowy Ejército Popular Revolucionario, or People's Revolutionary Army, which has pockets of support among peasants in several of Mexico's central and southern states. When the leaders of the Ejército Popular declared that their forebears included Florencio Medrano Mederos, reporters on both sides of the Mexican-American border asked, "Who was he?"

During the late 1970s, the states of Morelos, Guerrero, Oaxaca, and Veracruz were the scene of an ill-fated insurgency, led by Medrano, aka "Tío" (Uncle), aka "El Güero" (the Blonde). During that era—prior to the guerrilla outbreaks in Central America—both the Mexican and the American press stood in awe of Mexico's government and leaders. Medrano's movement was clandestine, with no secure turf, as in today's Chiapas; covering it was dangerous. For these reasons, the trajectory of Medrano's movement was the subject of only a half-dozen journalistic reports. *Texas Monthly* and *Mother Jones* published articles, NBC filmed a land seizure, and Mexico City's daily *Excelsior* ran a feature story with photographs—and ultimately a notice reporting Medrano's demise.

Ramón "Tianguis" Pérez was a courier and agitator in Medrano's ranks. His first published work, *Diary of an Undocumented Immigrant,* tells about the life that he led for several years *after* the failure of the guerrilla uprising. The present work is the story of his youth in Medrano's shadow, but it is more than that: It is a guide to the causes of today's rebellions in Mexico, and a picture of life within them.

The chief issue of the guerrilla movement in Medrano's day, as Pérez explains, was the ownership of land. Mexican law at the time guaranteed the integrity of *ejidos comunales*—farms and other tracts of land owned, not by individuals, but collectively, by the residents of villages in an ancestral pattern that pre-dates the Spanish conquest. Yet the residents of such *ejidos* widely reported that land once theirs had been taken by agribusinessmen—most often, cattlemen.

The Mexican Constitution, in that day, also promised land to every citizen. Landless peasants petitioned for the division of great landholdings, for agrarian reform, and for land distribution—one of the goals of the Mexican Revolution of 1910. The authorities ignored their appeals. Medrano encouraged them to force the government's hand.

Another level of the conflict—still smoldering today—is, from an American point of view, ethnic. Mexico proclaims itself a *mestizo* nation, the product of the blending of Spanish and Indian cultures. But as the Zapatistas have made clear, for millions of Mexicans, ancestral culture is still basic. Spanish is a second language for Ramón "Tianguis" Pérez, a Zapotec, as it was for perhaps half of Medrano's followers.

Because his account reveals some activities that might yet be investigated or punished—and because the accuracy of memory fades with time—Mr. Pérez has concocted some of the place names and most of the names of people mentioned in this work.

Other variations come about from the problem of translation. The term *campesino* is formally equivalent to "peasant," for example. I have left it in the Spanish where possible because for Americans, "peasantry" refers to an archaic European or Asian class, not to a group of people still present in the New World. The word *compañero*, which dictionaries equate to "companion," actually means something between the English "companion" and "comrade." I have left it in Spanish.

Americans today usually refer to the original inhabitants of our nation and their descendants as Indians or Native Americans. Mexican usage today prefers a term that translates as "indigene," a rare word in English, but one that I have generally chosen. The term becomes clunky when used to translate the name that a group of Medrano's followers took for themselves, the Indigenous Association for Campesino Self-Defense. "Indigenous Association" doesn't make much sense in English, perhaps, but "Indian Association" would contrast with the wording I've chosen elsewhere in the text, and the term "Native American" is confusing in a Mexican context.

Lastly, there's *chingar,* which, for better or worse, has no English equivalent, and carries too much meaning to translate: Understanding it requires a cultural depth that cannot be imparted by the printed page. Mr. Pérez would note that anyone who has been tortured knows what the term means—and he'd stress that, all books aside, ignorance and bliss are really the same.

Dick J. Reavis
Dallas, 1999

To the memory of Florencio Medrano Mederos

Behind me were all of the events, vague memories that bumped around my brain, one after another. Without really knowing it, I found myself seated on a bench in the Alameda Park in downtown Mexico City, recollections of Old Man Matías dancing in front of my eyes. There he was, sitting in front of Tío, with an anguished stare and a pained expression on his face. He had said in a desperate tone of voice, "Güero"—for that was another of Tío's names—"I've got the answer. Help me send that landlord into the other world!"

He had said that with such desperation that there was no need for him to explain. Tío had been aware of the Old Man's worries for a month or two. One morning the Old Man had come to Tío's shack to tell him about what he'd dreamed the night before. They were going to bury the Old Man, but he was still alive inside his casket. In the cemetery, four men had lowered him with ropes to the bottom of the grave, and he could hear the weeping of his family as they stood alongside of the hole. When the first spade of dirt hit his casket, he woke up.

Matías was about seventy-five, with completely gray hair that fell in tangled locks to his shoulders. He let his sideburns grow and combed them back so that they covered his ears. He was the leader of the *campesinos* who lived in that village, but it seemed that he'd grown tired.

"Güero, can it be that we're never going to win our struggle for the land?" he asked. "I don't know anymore, but lately I've felt a desperation that's hard to explain. I feel like I'm just going to burst from worrying about it. I'm getting so old that I hardly sleep, and when I do sleep, I have these nightmares. I dream that I'm going to die without getting any satisfaction, and my soul is going to be in pain. We've tried so many things and it's like our words were lighter than the wind. They didn't even cause an echo. The papers that we've drawn up, the petitions and denunciations, it's like they were written in vanishing ink. The way the officials act, you'd think we'd given them blank paper."

Old Man Matías always stopped by Güero's place on his way home from the fields—if he wasn't very tired, anyway. He'd always talk about his nightmares, which were all on the same theme: Somebody was dying and the land was still in the hands of usurpers. Tío sometimes made light of them, to lift the Old Man's spirits.

"My goodness, Matías," he'd say. "You either have to calm your nerves or find yourself a young girl for a wife."

But on the day of that visit, the Old Man had said, "I've got the answer." And Tío didn't argue with him.

Early one morning a few days later, two young *campesinos* came to the hut. In a burlap sack they carried two rifles and ammunition clips. They greeted me, but didn't mention their names. They took Tío outside to talk while I gulped down breakfast.

After a few minutes, Tío came back inside. He said that he had an errand to run, and that he needed someone to stay in the hut to wait for messages and to keep Old Man Matías entertained, in case he should come by. I agreed to wait.

Güero and the two *campesinos* didn't come back for more than four hours, and by then, Old Man Matías had come by. He seemed to have nothing to do, and, uninvited, decided to join me in waiting for their return. He took a seat where he always did, and said little as the time passed. But he seemed to grow worried and impatient, shifting about and looking outside the door. When the *campesinos* and Tío returned, they stacked their guns against a wall. They were out of breath.

"Matías, you can quit having nightmares now," Tío huffed, wiping the sweat from his face with a red bandanna.

The Old Man got up and went to where Tío was standing. He took Tío's right hand and looked him straight in the eyes. *"Gracias*, Güero," he said. His eyes were shining and there was a smile on his face.

"I would have gone," the old man added, "but I'm getting too old for such things."

About then, it dawned on me what had happened.

Tío put his hands on the Old Man's shoulders.

"Old Man," he said, "you've already done what you had to do."

But that day, March 30, 1979, it wasn't me so much as a sleep-walker tramping the streets of downtown Mexico City. I felt no urgency and wasn't aware that I was an obstacle to people who were making their way down the sidewalks in a hurry. A few of them dashed around me, saying things like, "Move over, you nuisance!" or "This guy must think he's taking a stroll in the park."

On the streets a never-ending river of vehicles passed like ants coming and going, but with one difference: These ants left pungent smoke in their wake. Some people, in a futile attempt to avoid inhaling the fumes, transformed their faces into grotesque masks that seemed to warn of impending attacks of epilepsy.

But I could have been hunched over in the chimney of a boiler without noticing. I just kept on walking among the throngs that passed on all sides of me.

"Everybody is going somewhere," I said to myself. "Some are more in a hurry than others. I know where I am going, too. But with me, it doesn't make any difference if I get there today or tomorrow, or if I ever manage to get there."

Passing by a little cafe, the aroma of food reminded me that I had gone two or three days without eating. I stopped, even though I didn't feel hungry. It was a little cafe, with perhaps room for four tables and their chairs. Except for a couple of flies that flitted from table to table, there were no customers. After I entered, a somewhat chunky and elderly woman came out from behind a curtain that covered the opening to another room. The news that her lonely business had a customer was sufficient to provoke the most splendid smile, but upon seeing how downcast I was, the woman's smile froze upon her lips, forming an ironic grin.

"How can I help you, young man?" she asked. Her expression was that of somebody ready to chase a stray dog out of the place.

I ignored her expression and took a seat. She moved her huge form to a shelf and picked up a sheet of paper that I supposed was the menu. But I didn't give her time to bring it to the table.

"I want coffee and *biftec a la mexicana*," I told her.

Because of the privilege that comes with being an only customer, the coffee was immediately served and the dinner wasn't far behind. I took some sips of the coffee and began to taste the sauce in which the meat was covered. The woman came and went from the kitchen and from time to time she looked me up and down. On one of her trips, noticing that I hadn't yet tried the *biftec*, she came over to the table, a little worried and a little curious, to ask me if everything was okay.

"Everything is fine, ma'am."

I tried again to eat, but my appetite was like that of a corpse on a birthday, and it was all I could do to drink the coffee. A little while later, I went to pay the bill and resume my wandering.

"Is something wrong, young man?" the woman said as she took the money.

"No, ma'am, everything is okay, don't worry. It's just that there are times when hunger escapes me."

After awhile, downtown was behind me. Crossing one of the streets, the screech of brakes and insistent honking made me snap back into consciousness. I was petrified for an instant. Another twenty centimeters and the driver would have hit me. With a wave of my hand, I showed appreciation for the driver's alertness, but that didn't save me from an endless litany of abuse.

Then the question came to mind, Did I really know where I was going? I was walking around in confusion, even though a few hours earlier I thought that I knew what I was doing. The night before I had left the town of Tuxtepec, Oaxaca, and I'd arrived in Mexico City very early. I had spent the morning and part of the afternoon wandering the streets of the city without knowing exactly what to do. The memory of the day before made me wander off again. Where had we failed? What was our mistake? I could recall perfectly the group of *compañeros* preparing to take over the land. It had been planned for quite a while. I also recalled Tío with his M-1 on his shoulder, heading up the group.

"Tío," I said, "I'd better go with you all."

"No, *compañero*, what I've given you to do is more important," he said.

"I could leave there later," I suggested. "Besides, Ernesto could take care of that business very well."

It was about four in the morning when they got ready to make the trip.

Tío was dressed as he always was: ill-fitting khaki pants, a cream-colored guayabera, and brogans.

"Tianguis," he said, a broad smile beneath his thick mustache, "when you come back, you'll go with us. Okay?"

Then, turning back to the group of *compañeros*, and tying a red bandanna around the back of his neck in the *jarocho* style, he asked them, "Are you ready, boys?"

Numerous affirmatives were heard. I said so-long to the *compañeros* who would go with him. I waited for them to leave and continued to watch them as they went down the trail in single file. A long walk was ahead of them.

That was the last time that Tío and I saw each other.

What should I have done? Who knows? If I had gone, what would have changed? Would it have served any purpose? Or is it that things had to happen that way? No, that couldn't be it. I remembered Tío's words: "Things turn out badly when they are badly done." But accidents happen, too.

"Accident!" I repeated to myself, believing that I'd found the answer. So that's what it was, a terrible accident.

The idea made me feel better. As I was considering it, I was crossing a park—the Parque México, I think. There I sat down on the grass beneath a tree.

But doubts came back to confuse me again. And the doctor? If we had gone looking for the doctor more quickly . . . But we had left Mexico City as soon as the doctor was ready. And we'd gotten in late. Yes, that was it, we'd gotten in late. We had waited, along with the doctor, for the contact who would take us over the mountains to the Rancho Cerro Fruta, a little settlement in the mountains where Tío was. It was more risky by the highway because the highway was occupied by federal troops. The contact showed up. He was a short young man with a round face and muscular arms. An old friend of mine. It was obvious that he was tired, but there was no time to rest. The doctor was picking up his kit, ready for the road, but our contact made a sign with his hand, indicating that he should wait. He seemed worried, and he was as silent as one of those posts that hold up a hut. He didn't say a word and our anxiety built up.

"What are we waiting for?" the doctor snapped. "Let's get a move-on!"

In reply, the contact man let some big tears roll down from his eyes, and his lips began to tremble.

"For God's sake, *compañeros,*" interrupted Doña Celia, directing herself to the contact man. Doña Celia was a bronze-skinned woman of about fifty, tall and thin, whose graying hair fell down over her back. She was the owner of the roof under which we were standing. A few months earlier, Tío had been her guest, too.

"Please say something!" she blurted.

The contact man, his eyes glazed over with the tears that streamed down his cheeks, stuck his hand in the right pocket of his pants and took out a golden-colored wristwatch with a gold-and-silver-colored metal band: a watch we all recognized as Tío's.

"Tío is dead," he mumbled, stretching out his hand to show us the artifact that proved he had come from Tío's side.

Doña Celia was stunned. She had been standing with one hand resting on the *metate;* now she let herself slide down into a sitting position on the bench that was next to a grinder. She pulled her apron up to her eyes and slumped, resting her head upon her hands. Her body shook as her cries escaped.

"Poor *compañero.* Poor man," she repeated over and over. "Only God can repay him for all he did and all that he suffered."

"We got here too late," the doctor muttered, shaking his head.

That same night he went back to Mexico City.

Later I saw Doña Celia come out of the hut with a candle in her hand. I washed the flower vases and went to get roses and fresh green leaves and branches. When the flowers were arranged in the vases, I put them on her little altar. They were like powerful guardians for the two framed photos that were leaned against the wall. Doña Celia lit a candle. She put it between the vases and then clasped her hands at her breast and said a silent prayer. The candle burned all night, casting a weak light, blinking and trembling as if it were anxious to slip through the walls of the hut, go outside and struggle against the darkness.

~~~~~

I lost myself in my memories again. A squirrel came down the trunk of a tree and leaped in little jumps across the grass. I followed it with my eyes until it disappeared among the shrubbery.

I realized that I needed to talk to someone. It would help me to feel better. Even hearing someone's voice would help. But that didn't promise to be easy. All of the *compañeros* had been taken into custody by soldiers.

My loneliness gave me purpose. The least that I could do, I figured, was go to the Centro de Comunicación Social (Social Communication Center). There they produced a news bulletin that paid a lot of attention to abuses of citizens' rights. Then I could go to *unomásuno* (One Plus One), the daily with the best reputation for critical journalism. Maybe at one of those places I could find somebody who could tell me what to do. But before I could go anywhere, I needed to bathe and change clothes.

That was another problem. Where could I go? Fabían had a room that he rented by the week, but it was best not to consider going there. He and I were *paisanos*. It hadn't been a year since he had come from Oaxaca and enrolled in the Universidad Metropolitana. I had stayed at his place, splitting the rent with him, before leaving Mexico City. I had kept stopping by, staying a night or two. Besides the fact that we were good friends, most of the furniture in his room belonged to my older brother, Benito, who had been living in the same apartment. My younger brother, Alfonso, had finished school and had now come to Mexico City for college. He had moved in with Fabían. Fabían knew that I spent most of my time working with the *campesinos*.

"Well, everybody has his own way of thinking," he said one time, "and my way of thinking is that I'm going to get my university degree."

"If anything happens, the police might look for me here," I warned him.

"If that happens, what should I tell them?" he asked.

"You should leave the house and not come back until things calm down," I told him.

So I couldn't go to Fabían and Alfonso's place. That wouldn't be following my own advice.

The only alternative was to go to my friend Benjamín's house. He was a Oaxacan who had lived in Colonia Escandón with his family until he got a job as a chauffeur to a family who let him have a couple of small rooms. He and I were about the same size and of the same complexion, and I was sure that he'd loan me a change of clothes.

From where I was, I knew that it wouldn't take long to get to his place. But two blocks before I arrived, I saw them. There they were, there was no mistaking them. And yet, preoccupied as I was by the bad luck of my *compañeros* who were in the hands of the police, and even though something in the back of my mind said, "Look out, those are police agents," at that moment I didn't even remember Tío's story of the rabbit. "Boys, walk with feet of lead," Tío had told us one time. "Do what the rabbit does. Before crawling into his hole, he looks and smells, and if he discovers something out of the ordinary, he goes on by."

One of them, with the body of a fighting ox, leaned with crossed arms and feet against the side of a car parked at the edge of the sidewalk. His head towered over the roof of the car and looked like something from Toltec days: curly hair and thick lips. His eyes were hidden behind dark glasses. He seemed to be scanning the entire street, but his gestures told me nothing, and no expression was visible behind his lenses. I figured that he had seen me, and that if I turned away, he'd chase me down.

Another cop was leaning against the lightpost. He had on sunglasses, too, and his were mirrored. He wasn't very tall because the newspaper he pretended to read left open to view only a rat-like face and his legs, clad in khaki pants. Had he been hiding behind that newspaper before I came into view? I didn't know. I hadn't been careful; I'd forgotten the rabbit routine.

I decided that the best thing was to play innocent. I went up to Benjamín's door, and was raising my right arm to ring the bell when something pulled at my back, with all the force of a talon. My feet lost contact with the ground before they were used as a handle to pull me on my stomach across the sidewalk. A heavy and powerful knee kept me glued to the ground while my arms were yanked behind my back. I heard the metallic snip of the handcuffs as they closed on my wrists, and about the same time, I heard a guttural voice at my ears: "Quiet, you son of a *pinche* mother, if you don't want us to take you to *la chingada* right here."

I was easily pulled to my feet to face a person who I remember cnly for his pot belly.

"We know who you are, so don't play dumb!" he said as he shot a fist into my stomach.

A tailgate opened and I was launched through it, to crash upon the steel floor of a pickup.

Far off I seemed to hear the voice of a child shouting: "Mother, some men are taking away Daddy's friend!"

It may have been one of Benjamín's daughters.

Then I realized that I wasn't the only one. There were two other bodies with hands cuffed behind their backs. The face of one of the bodies turned a little bit. It was Fabían! Fabían, who wasn't guilty of *anything*. I didn't say anything, but I tried to ask forgiveness with my expression, even though it wasn't going to do any good. Silently, the body turned its face away.

Nobody had to turn, and nobody had to tell me, for me to know who the other body was. It was my younger brother, Alfonso, who had been rooming with Fabían.

An agent got into the pickup, next to the driver. Two more climbed into the bed where we were; one of them was Toltec Head, the other, Rat Face. My head and Fabian's were at their feet. The pickup began moving away.

"So you feel real *chingón?*" Toltec Head asked.

None of us replied. Toltec Head raised his leg up a distance and, when it came down, the heel of his boot nailed me in the kidney. I felt like a worm getting its first peck from the chicken who's going to eat it.

"This is just the beginning," I told myself. "Hang on, because there's worse coming yet."

Weeks and months before, I'd tried to prepare myself mentally for what I knew was ahead. Being in the hands of cops like these, I knew, meant that you had to expect the worst.

"Where is Güero Medrano?" Toltec Head asked.

Tío was El Güero Medrano and also Florencio Medrano Mederos.

I asked myself if maybe they didn't yet know that Tío was dead, but I was sure that they had to know. I figured that Toltec Head was just asking to see how I'd answer. I didn't know how I should answer and he didn't give me much time to think about it. His boot was pressing on my temple, pushing harder and harder, grinding as if he were putting out a cigarette butt.

A sharp pain drilled through me, and I heard an echo in my head: "This is only the beginning."

It was only the beginning, but it had all begun two years before.

━━━⌇⌇⌇⌇━━━

Two years earlier, my older brother Benito and I were living in a pair of rented rooms in Mexico City's Agrícola Oriental district. Our dwelling was like most of those in outlying neighborhoods: One opened its front door and found oneself in a hallway, flanked by doors leading to rooms of unfinished cement block, roofed with sheets of asbestos. The shower, commode, and water pipes stood in one of the rooms, for the common use of all the inhabitants.

Our neighbors were from different parts of Mexico, and that's about all that we knew of them, because in the *vecindades,* the safest rule of conduct was to say little and know little, limiting one's conversation to formal greetings expressed in passing.

One of our rooms, which measured about two by three meters, we designated as a kitchen, though for cooking we had only a hotplate. The other room, about three by four meters, functioned as a living room, bedroom, dining room and study. We had two single beds, a closet, and a table with six chairs.

My brother was close to achieving the goal of most young people who leave the provinces for Mexico City after finishing secondary school. He was nearing graduation from a trade school, where he'd learned the electrician's trade. Without leaving his studies, he'd picked up a job as a maintenance man at an elementary school, and had ceased being a financial burden to our parents. His earnings had even provided him with a surplus for aiding me when I'd first come to Mexico City.

My brother didn't plan to stay in Mexico City after graduation. He'd go back to Oaxaca as soon as he could, and towards that end, he had used his vacations from school to develop contacts in the region that might provide him with an electrician's job.

When I'd come to Mexico City, I'd enrolled in a school that trained industrial mechanics. The school provided a three-year curriculum, but I finished only the first year before seeking work. My brother's assistance hadn't been sufficient, my parents had younger children to take care of, and under the circumstances, I'd thought it best that I find a full-time job. The school where I'd been studying had a good reputation, and that aided me in finding a job as a lathe operator in a factory that produced machines used to seal bagged and canned goods.

Maybe I lacked perseverance, but the truth is, studying and working at the same time, I soon got behind in my classes, and after three or four months, I decided that there was no point in continuing in school. I figured that further ahead, when our family's economic situation improved, I could always return.

My brother and I were living in these circumstances on the day that two of our *paisanos,* Flavio and Sabino, came to visit. Both had been classmates of ours, back in the village, and at the time were students in a forestry school on the outskirts of Tuxtepec, Oaxaca. Their visit lasted only a couple of days, but among the things we learned from them was that something was afoot in the tropical region where they were living, just below the mountains that were our home. A movement—whose size, depth and aims they did not know—had sprung up among *campesinos*. It was led by a man called "El Güero," who, our two informants said, was a survivor of the revolutionary movements of Genaro Vásquez and Lucio Cabañas.

My brother and I didn't make much of the news, because for us, it wasn't big news. There had always been organizations of Mexican peasants; the newspapers were full of their doings. That this movement was lead by a guerrilla was not a certainty. People always make up stories: After the murder of Emiliano Zapata, didn't people say that they'd seen him riding his horse in the mountains of Morelos? My brother and I wouldn't have been surprised if our friends had told us that Lucio Cabañas himself was organizing in the region—but we wouldn't have believed it, either. The news that they brought was, to us, like one of the crime tales in the newspapers; one reads of things that happen in some distant place or neighborhood, never close at hand. We were working and the people around us were also working, and in a word, nothing unusual seemed to be occurring.

Then I lost my job. It happened one Saturday a few weeks afterward, when the company where I worked celebrated the Twelfth of December, the feast day of the Virgin of Guadalupe, the patroness of both Mexico and the company. The Virgin's image, housed in a large glass case in a corner of the factory, was given a new silk dress that day, and her altar was adorned with lights and decorations of crepe paper. The owners of the company invited a priest about sixty-five years old, who, dressed in his cassock and stole, used a work table for a homily and a mass. At the end of it, he blessed us all and sprinkled holy water over each and every machine in the shop.

As was the custom at the plant, the bosses that day toasted the workers with food, music, and drinks. The fiesta was about four hours old before the workers who had come with their families began leaving, begging their way out with handshakes and smiles. Those of us who remained, including one of the plant's owners, continued our toasts.

In his cups, a lathe operator named Octavio asked the owner, a tall, round-faced engineer, a question: "So, Mr. Engineer, when will the raise come?"

"Ah, so it's a raise you want!" the engineer said with a chuckle.

"No, boys," he continued, in a more serious tone. "You should take into account that we're a new enterprise, and we're a Mexican enterprise. We have to apply ourselves in order to grow. When we do, then we'll see about raises."

"But listen, Engineer," Octavio argued. "You're paying me little enough already. I'm worth more. The company is exploiting me in an ugly way."

The engineer looked at him with an offended and accusatory expression. "Well, go wherever you want. Just see if you can find a place where they don't exploit you."

"As for us," he continued, now addressing the whole group and speaking in our name, "we'll go on working, all of us together. 'Onward and upward,' just like President Luis Echeverría says, because just like our next President, José López Portillo says, 'The solution is all of us.'"

"What's all of this?" interjected Octavio, visibly upset because the engineer was practically ignoring him. "The truth is, one thief is going to leave the presidential palace, and another is going to enter. There isn't going to be any 'onward,' or any 'upward,' or any 'solution' either. That's all bullshit."

"What are you, some kind of rebel?" the engineer exclaimed. "Well, you're fired, that's what. Adrián!"

Adrián was the factory's doorman. He had only to raise his glass to announce his presence.

The engineer pointed at Octavio and told Adrián not to let him into the plant on Monday.

Octavio looked into the faces of his co-workers, hoping for some support. It was pretty clear that he hadn't intended for the conversation to end as it had.

"Engineer," I said, "you can't fire this guy just for defending his point of view."

"Oh, so you agree with it!" the engineer retorted. "Then you're fired, too."

After that, nobody said anything.

We didn't believe that the engineer would follow through on what he'd threatened, but when Monday came, Octavio and I were halted at the door. Adrián went back to the office and returned with our pay.

"Here's what is owed you, and the engineer says thanks," Adrián told us.

I didn't go home for Christmas that year. Instead, I spent all of December filling out job applications. Nothing came of them. January went by in the same way. Everywhere I went, I was told that if any jobs came open, somebody would notify me. In February, I decided that I might as well go home.

⋙〰〰⋘

The town that I come from, Macuiltianguis, is located on the side of one of the mountains that compose the big Western Sierra Madre range. The village lies two hours by highway from Oaxaca City, plus another hour's walking time over a dirt road. Because most of its houses are roofed with sheets of tin, from afar the village looks like a shapeless iron reflecting the sun's rays. From time to time I've thought that the pile of metal looks like the remains of a boat that shipwrecked, without Noah's knowledge, during the Great Flood, and that remained lodged on the slope of the mountain, threatening to come tumbling down with any great tremor that the future might bring. But the village has been sitting there for centuries, always in the same position, even though history didn't notice the town until a little more than four hundred years ago.

Generations and generations have lived in the village, through epochs of poverty and times of territorial conflict with neighboring villages so severe that they've led to armed encounters. There have also been times of bonanza. It was the destiny of my generation to live in the time of the town's disintegration.

It came about slowly, but the truth is that today as many of our townsmen live in Oaxaca or Mexico City, or the United States, as remain behind. Those who are still in the village must find a means of making a living besides growing corn. Some are merchants, others are woodcutters in the communal forests. Some are at times bricklayers, or carpenters, or plumbers. Those who are retired live mainly on what their children outside of the village are able to send.

Everyone in town is a farmer, but it's mainly a tradition, because they invest more in the planting than they profit from the harvest, and for the most part, what they reap isn't sufficient even to supply family needs: Ours are corn farmers who, before the year is out, wind up buying corn. In better times, it was possible to say that our people were the children of the corn. The reason why that's no longer true, most of the townsmen say, is that the land has been growing poorer, year by year.

During the boom times, harvests were so bountiful that families had to build bins in which to store their surpluses. Livestock contributed to the wealth, too. Horses could be counted on for long trips, burros were healthy and capable of carrying more cargo than today. Even the pigs grew fatter, giving more meat. The eggs that our turkeys and chickens laid were bigger, and in those days, every house had twenty or thirty chicks jumping around in its yard.

Because of all this, the old people say, villagers were stronger in those days. An elderly lady once told me, "In those days, any man could carry a hundred-kilo sack on his shoulders, without his knees trembling a bit. And we women could bear ten to fourteen children without losing our beauty or strength. Today, all we have are men and women made of plastic."

Back then, the villagers grew not only corn but also beans, wheat, and peas. In the semi-tropical area of the communal property, they had planted orange, papaya, banana and mango trees, and even a few acres of sugar. We even had a water-powered flour mill, and a set of experts who made *tepache,* a wine drawn from the maguey.

There was a family of shoe- and sandal-makers, and a family of saddlers who cured the skins of animals slaughtered in the village. On the outskirts of town was plenty of limestone. People built ovens to process it, and sold lime to the surrounding villages. Almost nothing was lacking; one woman even kept a tobacco garden. She rolled her leaves in corn shucks and sold her cigarettes in packets of a dozen.

But all of this was before the highway, when, to reach Mexico City, one had to walk for three days. In those days a few merchants made the trip, bringing products from the city on their return trips. Once one of them brought back a case of Pepsi-Cola: what a novelty! The soft drink was sold by the shot glass, not by the bottle. During fiestas, anybody who wanted a shot of Pepsi had to prove himself first by downing two shots of mezcal.

But when the highway came, with it came commerce and disillusionment with the village's way of life. Little by little, stores began stocking goods that came from the city—not only those that hadn't existed in the village, but such things as packaged beans, sugar, flour, and cigarettes. Little by little, the villagers quit producing those items that were sold in stores, where there was always a reliable supply—but one had to have money.

A time came when the pull of the land wasn't strong enough to keep people from emigrating. The first group went to California with the Bracero Program. Others went to Oaxaca City and Mexico City, especially the unmarried young women, who found jobs as maids.

It wasn't easy for those who left behind families and customs to venture into unknown places, and they didn't miss any opportunity to come back to the village, most importantly, at festival times. They went back and forth so much that before long, they didn't know, when they made their trips, whether they were returning home to the village, or returning home to the cities.

Although they grew accustomed to city life, a lot of them kept toying with the idea of returning to live in the village one day. One guy planned to come home to plant acres of avocados on the south end of town, but of course, his plan, too, was only a dream. His job as a night watchman at a hospital in Oaxaca City barely paid him enough to support himself, his wife, and their six children. Money that he could have saved for the project was gambled away on occasional tickets in the national lottery.

With the coming of the highway, a new form of work came, too. As the blacktop advanced, we began to see in every village a new form of evangelist, men who represented a paper factory located on the out-skirts of the town of Tuxtepec. Because they couldn't reach our villages by auto, they came in helicopters whose landings, with their great rush-es of dusty air, were an entertainment for young and old alike.

The emissaries came to offer all kinds of public improvements in exchange for our signing a contract that would give their company rights to cut our communal pine forests. They offered to pay an annu-al royalty, to give us sheets of zinc for roofing our houses, to build schools and medical centers. They even promised to pave our streets!

Almost everyone was enthusiastic, and our village signed a con-tract, ceding its timber rights for twenty-five years. They day of the signing a great celebration was staged. The company's representatives, who by then were known in town as Engineer This and *Licenciado* That, had made sure that there was booze enough for everybody. They had contracted a local band, and there was dancing and drinking until dawn.

Not long afterwards, the company brought its machinery for open-ing trails into the mountain. A new source of livelihood was opened, and many of our townsmen bought the necessary equipment: a big saw for felling trees and segmenting them into logs, and a hook for drag-ging the logs to the edge of the trails. After the logs were stacked on the trails, a company man would come by, measure their cubic footage, and issue a check.

But as time passed, the promises remained only promises. Don Carlitos, one of the most important older citizens of the town, summed up the company's attitude by saying, "They only want what we have."

He was then in his seventies, thin and of medium stature. He and his wife lived alone. His three sons were married and gone, and his three daughters worked as maids in Mexico City. They had sent him enough money to open a little corner store. He no longer worked in the fields.

Once when I went by his store to have a cold drink, I found him reading, as was his custom, a newspaper about fifteen days old, one of those he bought as scrap and used to wrap purchases for his customers. While he went to open the soft drink that I'd ordered, I began to read the newspaper that had occupied his attention. In big letters, it announced the opening of a highway in a rural part of Oaxaca. The usual celebration was held, the newspaper said, and its coverage emphasized a phrase from the speech of a governor's representative: "To carry progress to the most distant communities."

"Have you seen what it says there?" Don Carlitos asked me.

Then he picked up the paper that I was scanning, and through the eyeglasses that he wore midway down his nose, read the same phrase in a loud voice.

"You can't believe those politicians," he said. "This business about opening highways to bring progress is just a lie. It's just like the highway that they opened here. It wasn't because they wanted to bring us any progress, but because they wanted to take away our trees for lumber. They don't care about us a bit. They just want what we have."

The people who had been working in our village as lumberjacks barely made enough to get by. "What progress is that?" he asked.

It was that progress that became my life after finishing secondary school, before I went to Mexico City to study the machinist's trade. There being no work in the countryside, I had joined my father, logging for the paper factory.

〜〜〜〜〜

Whenever men wanted to work at logging, the village authorities would assign them a stretch of a trail that the company had already inspected, marking the trees that should be felled. The work was a feat of endurance. We carried food for a week: tortillas, instant coffee, refried beans, cooked rice, boiled eggs, and the like. Along each trail, the company had put up a wooden shack, where we slept.

The trees that had been marked were generally the oldest, some of them two meters in diameter. To fell the trees, we worked in pairs, one man on each end of the long, big-toothed saw. It was necessary to cut the tree as low to the ground as possible, and that meant that we had to work nearly doubled over. After a few minutes at sawing, a pain would start in one's back, about waist-high. The sawing went slowly and with every pull of the blade the sawdust would stream out, little by little forming a mound on the earth at our feet. From time to time the resin of the trees would thicken, slowing the cadence of the blade. Sometimes when my back hurt, I'd look into my father's eyes, hoping that he'd say that it was time to take a little rest. But he usually looked as tranquil as if he were sitting in an armchair, sipping a cup of steaming coffee.

Again and again, I'd study his face as he looked towards a tree's peak. It was a habit of his, just a habit, because before we started to cut any tree, he'd make his reckoning, figuring where the tree would fall, and figuring, as well, where it was most convenient for us to cut. I'd watched him do it so often that I wondered why it was that he was always looking up at the peaks after we'd begun our cutting, what it was that he was looking for up there. But his stare was perhaps something else, a stare that went beyond the body of the tree.

"Why are you always looking up while we're cutting?" I asked him one day while we were eating.

He smiled, as if to himself. "It's nothing," he said. "Just a way of distracting myself, so that I won't be looking at how slowly the cutting is going. It helps me to not feel the pain in my back."

"It's practically a sin that you haven't told me before," I gibed. "You should have told me when we began to work, because let me tell you, there are times when I feel like my back is going to split in two."

"You're just short of experience, boy," he told me. "When we start cutting, you shouldn't get in a hurry, because you'll only tire yourself out. Don't ask the saw blade to move faster than it can; don't be looking to see how far we've cut. Everything in its time . . ."

I afterwards put his lesson to practice, and it helped. In time, I came to feel a satisfaction when the tree creaked like a door on rusty hinges. After that first creaking, I knew, it would take only three or four more passes with the saw before we'd hear the crack and roar of the falling tree, bringing down branches and smaller trees as it crashed. Its fall could be heard for hundreds of meters around, and was always answered by the shouts of other cutters, cheering our triumph. Afterwards, there would be a rush of dust and chaff, forming a kind of halo in the instant of death. Then, little by little, everything grew quiet again.

Accidents were a part of the work. A flying chip from a wedge put out an eye of one townsman, and a falling log broke another's leg. Luckily, none of us had died, though there had been deaths in other villages. When someone got hurt, the company paid a miserly compensation.

On Saturdays, after measuring the stacks of logs, an employee of the paper company would drive us back to town, where envelopes with pay from the previous week's work awaited us. On Saturday nights, I got together with friends my age, including those who would later bring the message of guerrilla activity to my brother and me in Mexico City.

One of them was Simón, a short guy with strong arms. We had called him Circus Man since the days when he was a boy, because he'd learned to stand on his head and walk on his hands like a world-class gymnast. Another was the curly-haired Sabino, whom we called the Drone, not because he was lazy, but because he'd seduced a girl whose beauty had made her the technical school's Queen Bee. A third, Flavio, we called El Beodo, because leafing through a dictionary, one of our students had found that the word meant "a drunk," and Flavio had shown that he could hold more mezcal than the rest of us.

On Saturday nights we'd go from the center of town to stores that sold liquor by the drink. Or we'd go sit beneath an old ash, whose age we never knew, and talk about the girls who were still in town. Beodo would bring his guitar, and as the village was going to bed, we'd make the rounds of its streets, singing where girlfriends lived, or at houses where possible girlfriends lived, even at houses of ex-girlfriends with whom we wanted to reconcile. But nobody opened a door for us, or even a window, nor did they turn on any lights. The women we were pursuing may have been listening in their beds, but acknowledging our presence just wasn't a custom. Our rounds were praised only by barking dogs. But sometimes at village dances, though the young ladies were always accompanied by their mothers, one or another would seize the chance to say, "Thanks for the serenade. You sing really well." The thanks may have been sincere, but the compliment, we knew was a lie, or else what saved us was only the accompaniment of the dogs.

One night we were gathered under the ash, trying to sing, when a couple walked by. The street lights didn't shine brightly enough to show us who they were, though it was possible to see, by their silhouettes, that they weren't people from the village. We townsmen knew each other, even in shadows. The woman was tall and slender, dressed in pants and a sweater. The man was even taller. He walked with a swagger and his hair came down to his shoulders.

"Good evening," he said as he came past the place where we were sitting.

We were already a little bit lit and, therefore, in quite a loose mood. The woman didn't say anything as they passed. She merely glanced at us as they walked by.

"Welcome, welcome, you're at home," Drone told them.

The young woman smiled a bit at the greeting and grabbed more tightly onto her companion's arm. Then the guy with the long hair looked over at us and smiled broadly. He stuck his free arm out towards us to wave. They went into the darkness and we sat there, commenting to ourselves that the guy sure had a pretty woman at his side.

Other shadows passed in front of us, always with a greeting or quip. The old man Remigio came by and told us that it was time to go to our houses.

"Only chickens go to sleep when it gets dark," Beodo told him with impudence.

About an hour later, the same couple of outsiders emerged from the dark. They were conversing and laughing in loud voices, more animated than before. We figured that they'd gone to one of the stores and gotten drunk. Drone strummed his guitar and began singing with Beodo "La Que se Fue."

"That's the spirit, boys," the long-haired guy said. "Play it!"

Drone quit playing and Beodo quit singing.

"If you want, we've still got some mezcal," Circus Man said.

"Let's say hello to the guys," the long haired-guy said to his mate.

"Nooo, no, you've already had enough to drink," she told him. But her warning fell on deaf ears because he was already making his way towards us.

Close up, we could see them better. The woman was well-proportioned, with light hair that came midway down her back. We could see that she had a pointy nose and thin lips. He had an aquiline nose, was wearing jeans, sandals, and a red plaid jacket.

Circus Man took out the little black clay pot that he kept in a net-like sack and offered it to the visitors with a little clay cup.

"But keep on playing," the visitor said.

Drone raised his guitar to his chest, Beodo cleared his throat, and they resumed singing.

After they finished, introductions came, followed by handshakes. The woman's name was Diana, the man, Alejandro, and they said that they were married. The had come from a university to do the social work required of sociology graduates.

"Now, let's sing some more," the long-haired Alejandro said, extending his hand to ask for Drone's guitar. "But let's sing something with social content."

We didn't know what they meant. None of us said anything. A song of "social content"? What could *that* be?

The long-haired guy plucked the guitar's strings, deciding that they were all slightly out of tune. He tightened the screws on its neck until he was satisfied with the sound, then raised a knee, supporting his foot against one of the roots of the old ash tree. He balanced the guitar over the leg that he'd raised and asked for a drink of mezcal.

Although his voice wasn't that of an orator, he began to declaim the introduction to a song that I would later learn: "There are memorable dates, days that can't be forgotten. The night of Tlatelolco, eternally to be remembered. All of the mothers of the world, with their wombs rent and torn, with a deep moan curse the soldiers. Everything that is called fatherland, marches, flags, all coming unraveled in the mud. The second of October, ladies and gentlemen, history was split in two. The night of Tlatelolco, I quit believing in God. Don't believe that God was there that terrible night, or else he would have protected his children."

As soon as he'd finished that, he began to strum his guitar to a *bolero* rhythm, producing a sweet, melancholy sound. Drone, noting that somebody could produce real music with his guitar, studied the player's every move.

The man's singing voice was better than his speaking voice. His ballad was about 1968, about some kind of massacre that had happened in Mexico City.

When the singer was finished, Beodo passed around Circus Man's cup of mezcal.

"*¡Salud!*" Drone told the long-haired guy. "You're going to have to promise to teach me to play like that."

"Of course, I'd enjoy that," the long-haired guy said.

The long-haired guy serenaded us with several other of his songs of "social content," as he called them. But Diana didn't sing along with him, say anything, or drink.

After awhile, Drone asked for his guitar, put it to his chest and told the long-haired guy that he was ready for his first guitar lesson.

Circus Man, who usually sang with Drone, was silent and pensive. The long-haired guy began showing Drone, first of all, how to tune the guitar, and the cup kept passing.

Circus Man came to my side and whispered.

"Did you understand his songs?"

"No, the truth is, I didn't. We'd have to ask him, wouldn't we?" I said.

"Naw, we can't do that. He'd just think that we were ignorant," Circus Man told me.

But after a while, Circus Man interrupted the visitors.

"Listen, can you tell me what is all of this about the coconut workers and the *tlatelolcos* and the tenth of June and the second of October? What's it got to do with songs of 'social content'?"

"You dudes don't know?" the visitor asked. "Man, you must be really disconnected. The second of October, 1968, was when President Gustavo Díaz Ordaz and the federal troops murdered hundreds of students in Tlatelolco Plaza in Mexico City. On June tenth of 1971 there was another repression by the government against the students; and the coconut workers, over in Acapulco, were also repressed for defending their rights."

That night the long-haired guy sang some more "songs of social content," and he and Drone agreed to get together for guitar lessons during the weeks when the long-haired guy would be in town.

But nothing more than that came of our introduction to college radicals.

———※※※———

Sometimes Drone, Beodo, Circus Man, and I would get together at Don Carlitos's store. The old man was a voracious reader, always ready to devour any written word that crossed his path. Sometimes he'd be so buried in his readings that he wouldn't notice when people came. Kids would take advantage by grabbing the candy he sold, then running out before he knew that they were there. His children, however, took notice and moved all of the merchandise onto shelves at the walls, putting the candy in a glass case that only he could open.

He was always glad to have the four of us in his store because, besides spending money there, we paid attention when he launched into speeches about the meaning of life. To tell the truth, he was the only person in town who made us think about anything beyond daily chores and drinking.

Don Carlitos had read the Bible cover-to-cover, but he said that he was an atheist.

"Boys," he announced one time, "how many times have you heard people say when they make some kind of mistake, 'Well, we're human beings and we make mistakes because we're not perfect. Only God is perfect'? Well, that's nonsense! A man is going to learn from his mistakes. Mankind is going to perfect itself, on the basis of learning from errors. The greatest inventions of the world were made after lots of errors, and it seems like mankind is never going to quit learning, because as soon as we learn something, we also learn that there's more that we don't know.

"If it's true that God made the world, He has my respect, because a lot of things are well-made. The human body, for example: Every organ works in coordination with another. In nature, little seeds grow into big, impressive trees. All of that and more is true, but still, I can't accept that God is perfect. If He exists, He's as imperfect as the world that He made. Because if this world were perfect, there wouldn't be so much inequality among men.

"The people who say that He's perfect are the priests, and they do that to justify their own errors, according to their own interests. This business of Heaven and Hell, I'll tell you, is just an invention of the Church, because I've read about the early followers of Christ, and they preached the true doctrine: equality among men, that we should help one another. That's the reason why the powerful men persecuted Jesus in his time.

"Sure, I know that among this mountain of false priests there have been some true ones, like Don Miguel Hidalgo y Costilla and Don José María Morelos y Pavón. They were true Christians, and there are a few of those. But the rest are only out to make money from the people."

Don Carlitos talked rather slowly, and he acted as if what he was saying was simple, as if its truth were obvious.

"Even with all of that," Beodo said after the lecture that Don Carlitos delivered, "you sell votive candles, don't you?"

"Well, yes, but everything has its explanation, young man," Don Carlitos said. "I didn't always sell them, but the sisters would come by asking for them. They growled at me and went to other stores, and finally, I had to attend to their needs. Remember that I'm a merchant and a merchant is a materialist. Beyond that, even if I didn't sell candles, do you think that the sisters would become atheists? It's just like with you. If I didn't have beer or mezcal in the store, would you quit being a drunk?"

〰〰〰〰

It was to this town, and to this life, and to figures like my dad and Don Carlitos that I returned after my failure in Mexico City. But my old friends, Circus Man, Beodo, and Drone, were gone. They had gone to forestry school in Tuxtepec. After a few days at home, I went to visit them.

Tuxtepec is a valley town. Its elevation is about fifteen meters above sea level. My village, by contrast, was at about fourteen-hundred meters. The road from the village to Tuxtepec winds like a snake in a continual descent that, by bus, takes about four hours. There's not a stretch of straight road in the whole hundred-kilometer trip.

As the road descends, it leaves behind the panorama of pines and comes into a flat region of jungle-like vegetation, short trees among tall ones, vines, and canebrakes, a seemingly impenetrable wall of greens and yellows. Its impossible to walk through this area without a well-honed machete and, most of all, a lot of strength. As the vegetation becomes thicker on the downward slope, the temperature rises, too. It's like going into the spout of a steam kettle. The heat turns you to soup and you sweat without doing any exercise.

On the edges of the highway stand isolated houses, shacks of wood with peaked, palm-thatched roofs. Almost invariably, the roadside houses stand in groves of banana, coconut palm, or *chicazapote* trees. This is the part of the country known as "The Valley of the Miserable Ones," the place where President Porfirio Díaz sent his enemies to work until they died.

The residents of this tropical zone are bronze-skinned, but their complexions seemed nearly transparent, as if sweating had that consequence. The men wear palm-leaf hats with high crowns, like their peaked houses. Most of them wear sandals, their shoes being reserved for trips to the cities and dances.

The land is as fertile as the climate is hot. The *campesinos* in the fields have to be always ready with the hoe and machete, lest their crops get overtaken by weeds. With care, nearly everything grows profusely: corn, chiles, oranges, tangerines, bananas, and even rubber trees. There are extensive plantations for pineapple and sugar cane.

My three friends were living in a *casa de vecindad* on the edge of Tuxtepec, an improvised place with walls of raw cement block and a roof of sheet zinc, a big rectangle divided into rooms about three by four meters in size, with doors made of unfinished lumber, doors whose only locks were a pair of eye bolts. The only furniture that they had in their room was a table of unpainted wood, stacked high with texts and notebooks, and two chairs. In one corner of the room a red plastic cord had been stretched to use as a clothes rack. In another corner their *petates*, or straw bedrolls, were rolled and stacked.

As I chatted with them, Drone asked me if I remembered the story he'd told me in Mexico City about the guerrillas.

"Sure," I told him, concealing my skepticism. "You said that there was some guy called 'El Güero' who had stirred up the people around here."

"Well, tomorrow we're going to see him," Circus Man told me. "You can come along if you want."

I was going to answer with sarcasm, but when I saw the seriousness that had beset them, I understood that they were telling the truth. Their manner wasn't like that of someone preparing for some adolescent prank, or to serenade a potential girlfriend. I took into account that we'd always been friends, together in nearly everything, and it seemed that I had no good reason not to accompany them.

But Beodo saw that I was pausing before giving an answer. "*Cabrón*," he scolded me, "this is serious business. We're preparing something heavy."

"Something 'heavy,' huh?" I said. "Well, we'll see tomorrow."

Fifteen minutes after the appointed time, an old Ford pickup pulled up outside of the rooms. There were patches of rust here and there on its body, and hardly a speck of its original light blue paint remained. Its cargo section was enclosed by wooden slats that had been painted a canary yellow, though in many places the wood was worn away by rough use. The truck looked like a bull that had survived many fights: scratched and scarred, maybe, but still strong.

The driver didn't get out. He had a round face, high cheekbones, snaggled teeth, and a dark complexion. Drone donned a baseball cap and then locked the door behind us, although it was hard to tell why. The safest place is where there isn't anything of value, and his room was one of those places.

"I want to introduce a *compañero*," Drone said to the driver.

He leaned across the cab and stuck his hand out the window, saying, "Good morning, *compañero*."

In that moment I had become a *compañero*, and the driver had become mine. I got the impression that the word *compañero* signified a pact, a commitment, and at the same time, an anonymity, because Driver (as we began calling him) neither told me his name nor asked for mine.

"Have you eaten?" Driver asked us. "There's a long road ahead."

Circus Man nodded.

Drone and Beodo got into the cab, next to Driver. Circus Man and I stood up in the back, holding onto the wooden rails. Pretty soon we were leaving the city behind, going down a paved road as straight as a ruler, surrounded by sugarcane fields. Before long we came into foothills and zones of pasture land.

After about two hours, the pickup left the paved road to head down a road that, though covered with gravel, seemed to have been an old creek bed. The pickup moved forward slowly, sometimes straining to advance, and creaking and bumping with every twist, drop, and peak in the road's surface.

We came to a village of widely scattered huts, made, like others in the region, of wood with palm thatch. On one edge were some small buildings of cement block, under construction, apparently, as substitutes for the *palapas*, or palm-thatch huts, that I took to be schoolrooms. Not far from the school was a bigger building, still lacking windows and doors. A chapel was obviously being built; a wooden cross, freshly painted, rose from the peak of its roof.

The climate was hot and humid, but the area's jungle-like vegetation was thinner there. The foliage had been burned and cut to create pastures: Pockets of the old ground cover survived in little ravines and niches. Here and there the charred trunks of old trees remained. The village was an *ejido*, or communal farm, called "El Porvenir," meaning The Future.

Driver parked his old Ford in the shade of an oak, said something to Drone in a low voice, and then disappeared into the settlement.

"Let's see if we can find some cold drinks," Drone said, pointing to a little store in the front of a house about twenty meters away.

The storekeeper was a man in his fifties who wore a cotton shirt and seemed as at peace with the humid heat as a little boy with a piece of candy. After serving us at his counter, he leaned forward on his elbows and stared at us with distrust.

I took the bandanna out of the back pocket of my jeans and began to dab at the sweat pouring from my neck and face. I looked as if the drink that I was gulping wasn't even reaching my stomach.

"You look like a guy who has just finished running a kilometer," Beodo said. He and the others were used to the climate. Only their foreheads and upper lips showed beads of sweat.

While we were waiting, Circus Man and Drone began discussing the steps necessary to solve a calculus problem that they'd failed to crack the day before.

The storekeeper, still staring at us, seemed uncomfortable with their talk.

"Where do you come from?" he asked Drone, who was standing nearest him.

"From Tuxtepec."

"And you, just how long have you lived on this *ejido*?" he asked.

Drone, having already glanced around the village, knew that it was a relatively new settlement.

"I am one of the founders of the *ejido*," the storekeeper said with obvious pride.

He said that the *ejido* had been formed about fifteen years earlier, by people from neighboring villages. The *ejido* was only now petitioning the authorities for the maintenance of a grammar school, because only recently had its school-age population become numerous enough to qualify for federal support.

"And how is your business going?" Drone asked, just to keep the storekeeper occupied.

"Well, I'm not the only one who has a store here. There's another one, about ten houses away."

About this time Driver came into the store. He ordered a soft drink and downed it in four long gulps.

"Sir," he said to the storekeeper, "can I leave my pickup with you? I've got some business to attend to. I'm a foxglove buyer, and I'm going to show these kids where the herb is worked and grown. They're just students who want to make a few cents, and I thought that I'd show them how, don't you think?"

The storekeeper seemed to accept the explanation and to relax a bit.

"Don't worry about it," he said. "We'll keep an eye on your pickup, even though there's not much need. Here nobody steals."

"I guess you're right," Driver said. "In the little towns it's not as bad as in the cities, and besides—if they do steal it, nothing is lost, is it? It just gets a new owner!"

The storekeeper laughed at the reply, though it was a traditional one. But it had worked to overcome his distrust.

Circus Man paid for the drinks, we said thanks and left the storekeeper among his merchandise like a frog sitting on a rock and waiting for a fly to pass.

We walked down what passed for the main street of the village until, at the edge of the town, Driver led us into a shack where a *campesino* of about forty-five received us. He shook hands with each of us before closing his door, then motioned for us to take seats on some tree trunks that had been hollowed-out in the form of chairs. The floor of his palm hut was of packed dirt, recently swept: The marks of a broom were still evident on its surface. On one the hut's walls, about halfway to the roof, a boombox stood on a shelf covered with an embroidered cloth. A half-dozen audio cassettes stood next to it. On the opposite wall hung a big calendar with a picture of a pure-bred dog. There were no other adornments or furnishings, except for a burlap bag full of dried ears of corn.

In the middle of one of the other walls was an entryway without a door that led to another room. A young *campesino* about twenty, dressed in jeans and a faded yellow polyester shirt, came out.

"Good afternoon," he said, with a quick smile.

A plastic hat, its fibers made in imitation of palm, was in one of his hands. He looked around until his eyes came to rest on the driver.

"So these are the student types?" he asked as he pulled the hat onto his head.

It was as if he was asking, "So these are the puppies?" The *campesino* wasn't much older than we were, but he regarded us with a certain air of superiority.

"Yes, *compañero*," Driver said with a touch of indulgence.

The *campesino* went over to the bag of corn, stuck his hand inside, and pulled out a black .38 caliber revolver. He raised it to the level of his face and flipped its cylinder open, making it spin as he peered at it. With a flick of his wrist, he then made the cylinder snap back into place. He passed the pistol behind his back and stuck it into his waistband.

"Let's go!" he said, like a schoolteacher inviting her children to recess.

We went out, with the young *campesino* and Driver in the lead. As we left the yard, I saw that the older man who had received us had come out and was stacking logs to make a fence. He waved to us as we passed. Before long we were heading into the jungle, walking down a narrow trail. All I could see of the young *campesino* was his back, the butt of his pistol protruding above his waistline. Driver was carrying a machete, still in a leather sheath, that he'd picked up as he left the house. The sheath was of the kind that is usually strapped around one's waist, but Driver was pot-bellied, and so he kept the machete in his hand. A belt drooped downwards from the sheath, bouncing off the ground with the rhythm of his steps.

"Give me the machete," the young *campesino* said. "Your belly is enough for you to carry."

"I'm a driver, *cabrón*, and a driver who doesn't have a pot gut isn't any good," he gibed.

In the middle of all of that brush, it seemed that there was a constant, if invisible, vapor of steam. After an hour of our trek, even the young *campesino's* shirt was wet with sweat. The faces of Driver and my friends were red from the heat, and I'd already had to wring my bandanna a couple of times. The terrain was nearly flat, and that was of some little comfort, because it was difficult for our lungs to fight against the heat and humidity. After a while, I quit sweating. My legs felt warm, and in my face and forehead I could feel blood pumping.

Every now and then, the land would take a little dip. At each dip, the vegetation was thicker and of a darker green. As we approached each one of the dips, I hoped that we'd cross a creek or a spring—anything with water. But all of the dips were dry.

Nobody said anything about being thirsty, and nobody complained. We were all afraid of the scorn of the young *campesino*, who advanced at a steady rate. If he could do it, we figured, so could we. None of us had brought water.

In our village, Beodo, Circus Man, Drone and I had become accustomed to hard work and long walks. But one gets out of shape sitting in classrooms, and the city is no place for fitness either: One only has to walk a block or two to the nearest bus stop. Factory work can be physically taxing, but I don't think that it conditions the body. In the cities, exercise is essentially an activity apart from daily life, whereas in the countryside, the two go hand-in-hand. In the country, if you're not in good physical shape, you can't work, and that's almost the same as saying that you'll die of hunger.

"How much further is it?" I finally asked the young *campesino*, after scurrying to catch up with him.

"Ah, it's not much. We just have to get to the riverbank," he said in a tone that made me think that we were only steps away. "You student types," he added. "I guess you've already gotten tired on me."

He looked around at Driver and at each one of my friends. And then he laughed.

"Don't get discouraged. We're almost there. We just have to get to the riverbank," he repeated.

"Yeah, we know that," Circus Man whispered to Beodo. "The only thing is, how far is it to the riverbank?"

The young *campesino* heard the remark, and laughing again, said, "We're not far now."

I asked myself how I'd gotten into a situation like this. I could as easily have been sitting on a bus to Mexico City—maybe even a bus with air conditioning. Nobody had sent me out here; my curiosity had brought me. My friends had told me that this was serious business, and now I was beginning to believe it.

It was a new situation for me. First of all, here I was a *"compañero,"* without the name that my parents had given me at baptism. Nobody had asked my name. Driver was another *"compañero."* The young *campesino*, he was a *compañero,* too. Nobody had introduced himself by his true name. All of us walking this trail in the jungle were *compañeros.* Only I and my townsmen knew what names to call each other.

Then, at the store, we'd had to conceal our purpose and lie to the storekeeper, who was practically dying to find out who we were and what we were up to. We were hiding ourselves.

We were on our way to meet a man who organized *campesinos*. Even in the city there were signs put up by organizations of peasants, the CCI, UCI, UGOCM, and so forth—all of them with the letter C standing for *"campesino."* But the *campesino* leader that we were going to see had *his offices* in the depths of the jungle.

Then there was the young *campesino* who led us, his pistol bouncing around in his waistband. In the village that was home to the three of us, when somebody went into the forests, if he had a gun, he'd put it on his shoulder, in case a rabbit or a dove went by, or with luck, maybe even a deer or a badger, whatever animal would complement a plate of beans. But at home our guns, rifles, and shotguns—those were for hunting. The young *campesino* didn't seem to have that in mind.

As we went along, all of us must have been thinking, as I was, of other times and places, anything to distract from the heat.

After a while, Beodo said to the young *campesino*, "Well, listen. Back in the village where we met, I saw a couple of children, and few men and women, but the girls? Where were the girls?"

"Damned student types!" spat the young *campesino*. "Do you think that we're going to let our girls parade through the streets just so that you can look them over? They're practically under guard, helping their mothers with the household chores. Only those of us who live there know when and where to find them. Damn student types!"

At last we came to a creek that crossed our trail. It was an arm's length across and its water was perfectly transparent. Circus Man threw himself down on his knees to drink from the middle of the current.

"Careful," the young *campesino* warned. "I don't want you to get spasms. As hot as all of us are, to take a big drink could kill you. If you want, wash yourselves, but before you swallow any water, let it sit in your mouth until it warms up a bit. Quench your thirst, but don't drink your fill because there's still a bit of a walk ahead of us."

We did as he said, wetting our faces, our hair, even our shirts. Then we sat down to rest a bit.

The sun had gone down by the time we reached the riverbank. The river was about fifty meters across, and it made a sound like rainfall. Its surface, a patchwork of tones of black, imposing and somber, looked like an undulating sheet of steel.

We had to wait about half an hour before we sighted the boatman. He was coming from the other side of the river with a passenger aboard. I watched as he crossed. His vessel was a canoe, about four meters long and ninety centimeters wide. From its form I judged it to be of one piece, probably hollowed-out from the trunk of a big tree.

The boatman was a middle-aged man. His pants legs were rolled up above his knees. He wore nothing from the waist up. To propel and guide his canoe, he used a long pole that he stuck into the river bottom. When he reached our bank of the river, his passenger got out and paid him, saying something in a language or dialect that I didn't understand. The boatman responded with a monosyllable that I couldn't make sense of, either. He didn't get out of his canoe, but just stood straight up at one end, supporting himself with his pole.

Without saying a word, the young *campesino* went down the two dirt steps between the bank and the canoe and stepped inside it. Driver followed, and then the rest of us. Driver motioned that we should sit on our haunches so that the canoe would quit bobbing in the water. When all of us were hunched-in together, I got the feeling that we were new-born ducks whose mother was going to teach us to swim.

The boatman stuck his pole into the river bottom and pushed, three separate times, to make his canoe turn 180 degrees. With a few more pushes we were well into the river. The current beat against the sides of the canoe, sometimes making a sound like that of boiling water, sometimes a lapping sound more reminiscent of those of a dog licking his wounds.

It wasn't long before we got to the other side. Driver asked the boatman what we owed him. He answered with a number and said nothing more. Perhaps the silence of the river had infected him.

Then we walked for about twenty minutes among the brush, until we came to a place where huts were built in the same style as the one where the young *campesino* lived: walls of a series of skinny sticks, triangle roofs covered with palm.

From the cracks between the sticks in the walls, in vertical shafts like curtains, came reddish-yellow lights that no doubt were from household hearths. Here and there we heard the voices of women or children, but because we were distant, we couldn't make out what they said. At almost every step dogs barked at us. In the fading sunlight, they were only dark blotches.

We passed maybe a dozen houses, until we came to one on the edge of the settlement, beyond which was nothing but brushland and impenetrable darkness.

A silhouette stood out against the weak light that came from that house. It was the figure of a thin man, tall, and wearing a hat. On his left shoulder was what I supposed was a rifle. He made no movement. Driver and the young *campesino* walked up to the silhouette and shook hands with him. When the rest of us followed up to the place, we were introduced to the silhouette, who also called us *"compañeros."* We all shook hands with him.

"Come on in," the silhouette said. He turned on his feet and led us inside the hut.

From the outside, Güero's place was only a big rectangular hut. The center of its largest room, perhaps six by eight meters, was illuminated by a gas lantern. At least two other rooms branched off from the big one, a kitchen, and another room whose entry was covered by a curtain. There was probably another room at the far end of the big one; we couldn't see it in the half-darkness, but we heard voices coming from there. There seemed to be three voices, to judge by their timbre. One of them, a thin, clear voice, spoke most often. A fuller voice spoke only short phrases. The third speaker had a high-pitched tenor's voice, the sort of voice that can't speak in secrecy.

Around the walls someone had stacked tree trunks here and there and laid between them a set of crude, hatchet-hewn boards. These served as benches. Nothing adorned the walls except a length of rope hung from a nail.

The silhouette that had invited us into the hut disappeared into the darkness as soon as we entered. Out from the kitchen came a young, thin woman of short stature. Her straight, shiny black hair fell to her shoulders. Her nose was *afilada*—narrow and pointed. She wore jeans and a checked blouse and high-heeled boots. The young *campesino* introduced us to her, and she gestured for us to take seats at the wall.

"They've come to talk with Güero, haven't they?" she said to the young *campesino*.

"Yes," he told them, "these student types want to talk to him. The good thing is that they made it here, but they barely did. They fainted on the trail," he said with his sarcastic smile.

She brought each of us a cup of coffee. The temperature had cooled a little, but was far from chilly outside. The hot, sweet beverage restored us a bit. Then she asked if we had eaten. Nobody said anything. We just looked at one another, trying to discern if anyone was brave enough to say that we were hungry. Nobody had the courage, but she understood, anyway. Fifteen minutes later, sitting on the knees of each of us was a plastic plate of refried beans and eggs, along with a home-made tortilla.

"She's the wife of the leader," the young *campesino* said when she had left the room, going behind the curtain.

After they finished eating, Beodo and Circus Man stretched out on the benches where they were sitting. Within ten minutes they were sound asleep. Driver, Drone, and I began drifting into and out of sleep, too. After awhile the young *campesino* came and shook each of us by the shoulders. We gazed up and saw in front of us a tall and muscular man dressed in a guayabera, loose khaki pants, and work boots. He was smiling from beneath a mustache, big and thick like Zapata's. His skin was light and his short hair, auburn: undoubtedly, he was El Güero. The young woman was at his side, evidently as amused as he was that we'd fallen asleep. We were rubbing our heads and eyes, trying to summon alertness.

"You boys came in tired?" the smiling man with the mustache said. It was the same voice that we'd heard from the far end of the room, serious and clear.

The young *campesino* stood up and offered a handshake. The two men embraced.

"Tío," the young *campesino* said, "these student types and this *compañero* want to chat with you. They're from the Tuxtepec area."

"Welcome, *compañeros*," Tío said with a nod.

He greeted each of us in turn, shaking hands and embracing us and extending his welcome with phrases like, "How good that you've come to visit, *compañero*."

He asked if we'd had trouble on the road or trail, and asked if his wife had offered us anything to eat.

Driver asked what time it was. Tío looked at golden-toned watch on his left wrist. It was about eleven o'clock, he said. We had slept for nearly two hours!

The young woman went behind the curtain and came out a few seconds later carrying a roll of *petates* beneath her arm. She laid the roll at the base of one of the walls.

"Make yourselves comfortable as best you can. Rest up. Tomorrow we'll talk," Tío said, meanwhile rolling the *petates* out onto the dirt floor. "It doesn't get cold," he continued, "but it does get a little brisk in the early morning. Here in a minute we'll give you some blankets so that you can cover yourselves. I don't imagine that you expected beds, did you? When one is tired, just about anything will do."

We needed a rest. We had walked for eight hours, and we hadn't been prepared for a trek of that length. We hadn't expected a fluffy bed, but we hadn't expected to spend the night, either.

The Silhouette Man who had received us entered the room along with another man, who greeted us only by saying, "Good evening." Silhouette Man was carrying a rifle that was more massive than the .22

calibers that I'd seen; later I would learn that it was an M-1. The other man was carrying a shotgun. Both carried their guns pointing downward at the floor. They sat down on one of the benches and put their guns between their knees, barrels pointing upwards.

Silhouette Man was dark-skinned, about thirty, with a wispy mustache and small, sunken eyes. The other man was younger and fatter, with a long shock of hair over his forehead.

"Is there any news, Jorge?" Tío asked Silhouette Man. I was surprised that he was addressing somebody by a real name.

"No, there's nothing new," Silhouette Man said.

Then Tío asked about several people by their nicknames and Silhouette Man told him where they were. The man with the shotgun got up, went to another part of the hut, and came back with another roll of *petates*. Güero's wife brought blankets for us and we prepared for sleep.

"This man," Driver said, referring to Tío, "was the one who founded the Colonia Rubén Jaramillo in the state of Morelos. He was with Lucio Cabañas in the mountains of Guerrero and also fought alongside Genaro Vásquez."

"How do you know?" I asked.

"I just wanted you to know, and that's all I can say," Driver replied, cutting off my inquiry.

"No news," I said to myself, repeating it a time or two. That meant that there could be a time where there was or would be news. Those two guys with guns and the young *campesino* couldn't be the only ones who were involved. Some of the people that Tío asked about by nicknames were probably armed. It had been enough news for one day.

I went about ten meters outside of the hut to take a leak. Drone showed up for the same reason.

"Is this an armed movement?" I asked him. "Is this about guerrillas?" Certainly I knew that Genaro Vasquez had been a guerrilla. I'd seen a picture of him, wearing a jean jacket, a rifle at his chest.

"I don't understand it all very well, either," Drone said. "I knew that this was something serious, but I didn't know *how* serious."

What could be the news that Tío had asked Jorge about? Were they watching for the arrival of federal troops? I began to feel a little nervous, and I figured that my *paisanos* felt the same way. Just for safety's sake, I decided not to take off my shoes before going to sleep. I might need them to run, I thought. But run where? There was a door from the kitchen to the outside, an unusual feature in a hut like this. I was sure that it hadn't been put there for nothing.

"I'm going to sleep with my shoes on," I told Beodo.

"Me, too," he said.

Circus Man and Drone had stretched out on their *petates,* just as they were, without undressing. Driver had only loosened his shoestrings. The young *campesino* was the only one who had taken his boots off.

Despite my tension, it wasn't long before I was asleep.

I had a nightmare that night. I dreamed that I was in Mexico City working in the factory. It was a payday. I was walking towards the street where I always caught a bus to ride home. I noticed that a man with a thick neck was following me. I turned a corner and looked back, then turned another corner, and looked back again. He was stalking me. I watched him out of the corner of my eyes, and just when I was sure that he was going to attack me, I threw myself into the river of traffic, barely missing one car, then another, then another. When I got to the opposite sidewalk, I looked back at him and laughed because he hadn't been able to follow me. Seeing me laugh, he pulled a pistol and pointed it at me.

I started running, but I wasn't in Mexico City anymore. I was running through the countryside, and at my back I heard martial music and the tramp of boots. I ran until I came to the edge of an abyss and I was falling towards its bottom when I woke up and found that I was in the hut.

I must have grunted or spoken during the nightmare, because the man named Jorge raised his head and said, "What's happening to you, *compañero*? A nightmare, huh? Go back to sleep. Sometimes it is not good to eat before going to bed."

The sun had been up awhile when we awoke. The two armed men and the young *campesino* had vanished without a trace. Only Driver and my *paisanos* were in the room. Nobody seemed to be around except Tío's wife and a little girl who was playing with some chickens in the yard. Somebody had thrown some corn onto the ground, and as the chickens tried to peck it, she vainly tried to pick them up. Her skin was white and her brown hair was lightly curled. She must have been about two years old.

Güero's young wife introduced herself. She told us that her name was Silvia, and that she'd rather be called by any name than to be called *"compañera,"* or worse, *"señora."* She also told us that Güero had gone out but would be back shortly. She referred to him as Güero, not Tío.

"Which of you knows how to cook?" she asked while the five of us watched as she cooked some noodles in an aluminum pot. Her kitchen consisted of a big wood fire between four big posts that sat on a dirt platform of about fifteen centimeters thick. The tops of the posts weren't more than ninety centimeters high.

"I know how to cook, *compañera* Silvia," Drone told her. "But I only know what you might call high-class cooking, like baking a chicken, things like that."

"Well, we've got chickens here," she said. "All we need is an oven. Until you bring me one, why don't you turn the crank on this corn grinder? Another one of you can feed the corn into the machine." She said this without losing her sense of humor or turning away from her cooking.

The machine that she was talking about was a manual grinder made of iron. It was painted the color of aluminum and affixed to a post that was stuck in the ground. Its handle was about the height of Drone's shoulders. He began to crank it, while Driver put the corn into its mouth.

"Will another one of you do the favor of going for water?" she asked. "There, just outside, is a trail that will lead you to the spring. I'm pretty sure that you guys don't do these things at home, but here, *compañeros*, everybody has to help out. If the system has to be changed, one of the things that will have to change is that the woman can't be enslaved to the kitchen. Activities have to be shared."

"We're in complete agreement, *compañera*," Beodo said while he looked for the bucket to go to the spring. "But could you just not give us your lectures before breakfast? It's bad for people's health, you know. I'm going for the water before you start scolding us again."

There was nothing for Silvia to do but laugh. She even quit stirring her pot. Nobody had ever given her flak about the rights of women before.

Two of us were left with no chores to do, but we decided to take turns with Drone at the grinder and to relieve Beodo after he'd made a couple of trips to the spring.

All of the plates and cups in the kitchen were of plastic, and the few pots and pans were of aluminum. There wasn't one single dish of clay or glass or any delicate material. The kitchen utensils were cheaply made.

Three-quarters of an hour later, we'd all had a good breakfast.

"Now, *compañeros*, let's see which one of you washes dishes," Silvia said.

All of us had been helping each other, grinding and carrying in shifts. Nobody could say that somebody else hadn't worked, so that washing the dishes would fall to him. So someone pulled out a coin, and we flipped it to determine whose job it would be. The scrubbing fell to Driver.

Tío came in a little later. Silvia served him his breakfast and, while he ate, he busied himself by asking us where we came from and what we did. When he finished, he asked us to walk with him over to a piece of land where ground was being broken. Before we left, Jorge came in and joined the group.

We walked for about half an hour over what seemed to be a deer trail. Jorge took the lead, unsheathing his machete; from time to time, I could hear its metallic ring as he cut a branch out of our way. Tío followed him. I had thought that he was unarmed, but while we were walking, he bent over to move a piece of stone or wood out of the way, and I noticed a bulge beneath his guayabera, on the left side. The bulge had to be a pistol.

As we walked I asked myself what we would see when we got

where we were going. Was there a cache of hidden guns at the end of the trail? A training camp?

But my fears were unwarranted. We came to a place where a tractor was breaking ground. It pulled behind it an implement made of sharp steel discs. It cut down plants as high as two meters tall and plowed their remains into the dark soil. At some point, that piece of land, about two hectares in size, had been planted in corn, because dried stalks were in the overgrowth. At the wheel was a chubby man with dark skin and a burr haircut. He waved when he saw us walk up, but kept to his plowing.

"Our organization bought that tractor," Tío said. "It is being used to cultivate this land, collectively, by the *campesinos* of the settlement where we're living. We also let people who have private plots use it, if they'll contribute to its maintenance."

The tractor made two or three more rounds in the field and then it stopped. The driver climbed down, without turning off the motor, and came over to say hello. He was a tall man, about thirty-five, whom Tío called Valentín.

"Did you boys come to work?" he said to us as we were shaking hands. "Just say yes, because there's plenty to do."

Valentín explained to Tío that he had already finished breaking ground on two new plots and that before nightfall he'd be finished with the one he was working. Tío took us to see the other two plots. Several people were working there, cutting posts to enclose their new land.

About three hours later we were walking back towards Tío's hut on the same trail. When we came to a clear spot where leaves had formed a carpet on the ground, Tío said that we should stop to rest. We weren't tired, but we sat down on the roots of a big tree, anyway.

I lit up a cigarette. Jorge and Circus Man bummed from me.

"So you guys are students?" Jorge asked as he lit a match.

"Be careful about starting a fire," Beodo said, just to say something.

"What are you talking about?" Jorge shot back. "These woods are so wet that you couldn't set them on fire even if you had barrels of gasoline."

"Well, if we've got time to talk, *compañeros*—" Tío said, and made himself comfortable in the leaves, leaning back against a tree. He pulled his pistol out of his waistband and laid it down next to him.

It was a semi-automatic .38, blue steel. The pistol grips were of a silver color with figures in relief.

"I come from around Valle Nacional, Tío," Driver said. "I bring greetings from some of my *paisanos*. They want you to give them an orientation or an alternative, so that we can get justice. For more than ten years we've been filing papers with the Ministry of Agrarian Reform, trying to get our lands back. We've joined up with the Unión General de Obreros y Campesinos de México (General Union of Workers and Peasants of Mexico), the UGOCM."

Tío was sitting crossed-legged like Buddha. On his right knee he held his pistol.

"Ah, I've got it," he said to Driver. "The director of that union is the *Licenciado* José Francisco Miranda."

"That's right, Tío."

"*Compañero*," Tío said, "what you don't know is that this organization is subsidized by the federal government and the people who work with it do more to get the federal subsidy than to defend the interests of the *campesinos*. There are two-faced people, like this *Licenciado* Miranda, who is a descendant of a family of landlords in the Mazatec region of Oaxaca. They've been in that area about ten years, where the population is Chinantec, Mixe, and Zapotec. He came to promise them that he'd resolve all sorts of problems, from recovering the communal lands, to putting in roads, telephone lines, lights, and hospitals.

"Francisco Miranda," he continued, "is a political gunman for the landlords and *caciques*, from whom he receives, in addition to the federal subsidy, lots of money. He exploits the *campesinos* that he claims to defend. Francisco Miranda is a demagogue through and through."

His remarks were turning into quite a little speech.

"Used to be, at his meetings he'd shout to the four winds that that he was on the side of the poor *campesino*. He'd say, 'If a landlord dares to take the life of a *campesino*, I myself will see to it that ten landlords are killed.' The *campesinos* would even let their children go without clothes to raise the amounts of money that he charged for supposedly arranging their affairs. So if this guy is in your region now, you should unmask him, because the only thing that he's going to do is deceive and exploit.

"Tell me," he asked, "what has happened to the *campesinos* that he couldn't moderate? Haven't they turned up in jail on false charges, or been murdered by the landlords' White Guards and *pistoleros*? In the past ten years, there have been jailings and killings and people thrown off of their lands. Just tell them the name of any landlord or hired guns who have been jailed!"

"What would there be to say?" Driver replied. "All of that is true. *Licenciado* Miranda gets lots of money from the collections he takes up from the *campesinos*. Just for getting us copies of the Primordial Titles to our land he's asked for twenty pesos from every *campesino;* take into account that there are not just one or two hundred of us, but more. But if he can solve our problems, even if it's expensive, it will still come out cheap."

"Unfortunately the Mexican countryside is plagued with land-lords," Tío said. "Wherever there's a good piece of land, you'll find a landlord who has usurped the title. When they can't do it with trickery, and the *campesinos* won't give up their land, they invent false accusa-tions and have them thrown in jail. Or they call on their hired guns, and when they're least expecting it, the most militant *campesinos* turn up dead. The worst of it, there's never any punishment. All of these actions are encouraged by people in the government.

"Another way they do it," he continued, "is to corrupt the *campesino* leaders. We live in a system where the conditions in the countryside are semi-feudal. The *campesino* doesn't have the protec-tion of the laws, and a *campesino* like that had best seek help from somebody who stands in his shoes. Pretty soon he'll find that he's not just one, but two, and the two will become four, and the four, eight, and so on, until the group is big enough to take the solution of its problems into its own hands. Then they can make the landlords and the authori-ties pay attention to their demands.

"The peasantry has to recognize its friends and its enemies. That's one of the reasons why we've organized. The most conscious sons of the people have to take up the banner of struggle, to emancipate the *campesinos,* so that together we can permanently throw the landlords out of our communal lands and build a decent life like human beings, for us and our children."

Driver said that he'd try to take that message back to his village.

"And you, *compañeros*?" Tío asked. "What can you tell me?"

"In our village there are no landlords," I said.

"We name our authorities democratically," Drone told him. "Nobody puts them in office. We have a roll that assigns citizens of the village to office, by turns. If you're a policeman when you're young, for example, when you get older and acquire more experience, you're assigned to different posts, and you can even become mayor."

"The last time we had a killing for political reasons in our village was in 1945," Circus Man chimed in. "The only killings that we've had since have been crimes of passions and one or two suicides."

Beodo seemed anxious to speak. "We also don't have fights in town over political parties. When election days come, everybody has to vote. It's a requirement, as if it were important to us. We also don't have any conflict over religion. Everybody is Catholic."

Then Beodo told him what had happened years before, when a Protestant preacher had come to town, a suitcase in one hand and a Bible in the other. He came into the middle of town and tried to preach to the first person he encountered. As it turned out, that person was the chief of police. As soon as it was clear to him what the preacher's purpose was, the chief told him, "Boy, I'm giving you half an hour to get out of town. If you don't, I'll jail you. I'm not going to let you come in here and divide us. Things are fine as they are."

"My goodness!" Tío said, plainly amused. "So there are no problems in your village? Nobody is exploiting and nobody is exploited?"

In a way, it was true. The great division of wealth that he'd mentioned in other places wasn't a problem for us. Nobody in our village was rich. Sure, there were store owners and merchants, even one who had a truck for bringing his merchandise from Oaxaca City. But if he had great wealth, he didn't show it.

"Things that will benefit the whole village we organize in a collective way. We call it the *'tequio,'*" Drone added.

"Well, then," Tío said. "Then there's no point in making the Revolution, boys. We're so advanced that we already have socialism. Perfect! If I had begun in your town, we wouldn't be sitting here now."

We didn't know what to say. He was clearly amused, but we weren't lying about the way we lived. We didn't have any gunmen and there weren't any problems over ownership of the land.

"No, boys, the way your town chooses its officials is fine, and so is the collective form in which it works," Tío explained, speaking seriously now. "I understand that there are no landlords, probably because the land isn't very good. But how do you live?"

"Small-scale cultivation of corn, " Circus Man told him. "A lot of our people have gone to the United States as *mojados,* and others work for the paper factory in Tuxtepec, cutting trees in our communal forests."

"And the factory pays you well for the wood?" Tío asked. "Those who cut the trees have a decent standard of living? Do they have good benefits? They ought to live well, because besides being the owners of the raw material, they're selling their labor power. What benefits have come to your village since the paper factory started exploiting your woods?"

That was the point to touch. It had been twenty years since they'd begun cutting the trees, ever since the highway was opened. In 1956 the Secretary of Agriculture, without taking into account the interests of the owners of the command forests, through a government bank granted 185 million pesos, along with a concession, to the Tuxtepec company. The concession affected 271,000 hectares of forests that belonged to Zapotec, Chinantec, and Mixe communities in the Juárez Mountains and in Playa Vicente, Veracruz.

The men who worked as lumberjacks lived precarious lives. I remembered what Don Carlitos had said: "They don't care a bit about the people. They want what we have." The company wasn't paying the going rate for its logs, and its promises to provide medical care, support education, and improve our houses and streets had been just promises. Nothing had materialized.

But the woods, which once had virgin trees hundreds of years old, were suffering the effects of the logging, and every time the company sent in its machinery to cut trails, they had to go deeper into the forests, where virgin trees were still to be found. You couldn't see any improvement in the workers' quality of life. Their pay was miserable, and the work exhausting. What they earned was only enough to sustain them as workers.

In a general assembly in 1970, the village had decided to demand that the factory pay more for every cubic meter of wood that it took and that it also keep the promises that it had made in the beginning. It refused to pay more, pleading low profits, and it said that it was making efforts to honor its promises, but that we'd have to wait. Our political hired gun was *Licenciado* Hugo Lindo, a man with a round face and well-stuffed cheeks. His job was to get the village to back down from its demands. But the strike came anyway.

For the company, it was just an affair that affected one village. It didn't pay much attention. But the strikers named a commission to talk to the nearby towns. It didn't take much explanation, because those villages had contracts with the paper company, too. A month later, not a town in the mountains was turning over a single log to the company. But the company knew that none of the people in the villages could have much saved, and it gambled that we'd get tired and hungry.

The political gunman made the rounds of all of the villages and tried to divide the movement, but no deals could be made without the approval of each town's general assembly. A year went by and the strike held. The company, for its part, set up new contracts with towns on the Pacific coast that also had useful forests.

The towns that were on strike saw their hopes fading, and because our lands weren't as good as they had been in the distant past, a lot of people had to go to the United States. Before long we heard that one village had given in, without gaining anything, and three months later, another, until only four towns remained beneath the banner of the strike. Those four, including ours, hung on for three long years before giving in.

Even though not all of the towns held out, when the strike was settled, the benefits for all of them were extensive. The company increased the price that it paid for wood, though inflation during the three years had left us in almost the same state as before. The company provided sheets of zinc for people to use in roofing their houses. It began building what would become our medical clinic, and on every trail it built little shelters so that the loggers could take refuge in bad weather.

But it had been five years since then, and the situation of our townspeople wasn't much better. Our people were working on our own land, with our own implements, twelve to fourteen hours a day, to cut about twelve cubic meters a week, at about seventy pesos per meter. A team of two loggers earned about eight hundred and forty pesos a week, or one hundred and forty pesos a day—seventy pesos each. The daily minimum wage in the state was fifty pesos, for an eight-hour day, and that for labor only, without tools. The amount that our loggers were being paid was minimal in the extreme.

"You guys have before you a big enemy that has spread to other parts of the state," Tío said after we explained all of this to him. "Your job is to raise the people's consciousness. You have to build a stronger organization so that the next time you strike, it won't happen like five years ago. You need to see that your people know their rights and learn how to defend them. The villages that own natural resources ought to live well, but you've got a vampire feeding on you, and it will kill you if you don't defend yourselves."

We were impressed by what he said, and kept listening.

"Our job is to organize the *campesinos*, the workers, the students, and honest intellectuals who are willing to fight for a revolution in Mexico. We are based on the legacy of Emiliano Zapata, Don Miguel Hidalgo, Rubén Jaramillo, Francisco Villa, José María Morelos, and the others who have fought at the side of the people, with the people, and for the people—the working people, the exploited, the oppressed. We're for the workers who are exploited by the capitalists, and against the landlords who, with their White Guard gunmen, have dispossessed the villages of their common properties. We live in a Mexico with an underdeveloped capitalism in its cities and a semi-feudal system in the countryside.

"Our movement," he continued, "is also the result of a series of experiences like those of the *compañeros* Génaro Vasquez, Lucio Cabañas, and Arturo Gamiz, who offered their lives for the sake of the people. These *compañeros* deserve our respect because they died for their ideals. But they also made mistakes, and we have to learn from their mistakes. These *compañeros* believed that a small unit of guerrillas, Ché Guevara style, would be able to carry off a revolution in Mexico. That's not the way, because the guerrillas can't be disconnected from the people. A revolution has to be made by the people—that is, directed by its best children. That's why our idea is to tie ourselves to the people, so that we can teach them the ideal of struggle. They have to know their rights and know how to defend them against oppressors and exploiters and their servants."

Then he told us that he was a member of the Partido Proletario Unido de América (United Proletarian Party of America), the PPUA. He said that he'd make sure that copies of the party's program reached us. Half an hour later we were on our way back to the hut.

We were ready to go back. But before leaving, we had lunch. At the table were Tío, Silvia, Jorge, Driver, and the young *campesino*, who was to lead us back.

"These *compañeros*," Tío quipped to Silvia, "come from the sister Socialist Republic of Macuiltianguis."

The person who laughed the loudest was the young *campesino*, who was still calling us "student types."

"That's right," Drone replied in a joking tone. "We're here on a visit to the sister Feudal Republic of Paso del Toro."

On the way back, we spoke very little. Maybe everybody was trying to conserve strength for the long walk, or maybe each one of us was digesting what we'd seen and heard. The same taciturn boatman took us back across the river. It was a wide river whose surface was green, and in some places, gray. For about five hundred meters you could see the river, but then, at a turn, the foliage swallowed it again. At its edge, women were washing clothes on flat rocks. The water came to their waists, above which, most of them were nude. As we came near, they seemed to pay no attention, and they made no effort to cover themselves. Shame wasn't a part of their customs; nobody had taught them to be ashamed.

We were still on the trail through the woods when nightfall came. Only the frogs and the crickets broke the silence, and now and then, Driver, who from time to time would speak up, as if thinking aloud.

"This is the man that we *campesinos* need," he said. "He survived Genaro Vásquez and Lucio Cabañas. He must have a lot of experience. That man is a real revolutionary."

He turned his head toward Circus Man, who was walking behind him. "Just tell me: Who is willing to risk his life for the poor? Look, I've got a wife and children. I have to work so that they won't have to do without anything. I think only about them. Other people aren't my problem. I know that's selfish, I know that well. But how much of a conscience do you have to have so that you can live like Tío? He's got enough intelligence to make a living. He could do like *Licenciado* Miranda, who visits the countryside but has a home back in Mexico City. No, this guy is different. He's a real revolutionary. You can't doubt him."

Nobody commented on his reflections. But we could see that it was true. Tío was armed, and the people around him were armed, and that meant that he wasn't just anybody. He couldn't walk four or five kilometers, like anybody else, without having to watch his back. But he still knew how to joke around, unworried. He smiled like the simplest man, but when he spoke, he was convincing, very sure of what he was saying. He made us feel like he was a man we could trust.

"What you didn't see," the young campesino told us as we were getting near the end of the trail, "is that every day *campesinos* come from different parts of the region and they always invite him to their villages so that he can talk to the people directly."

We didn't have any idea about what we could do to help. We knew it wouldn't be an easy matter to organize our community. It was something that we'd have to think about. Beodo, Circus Man, Drone, and I didn't think that it would be such a bad idea to lead the towns into another strike against the paper company.

On the way back to Tuxtepec we talked about it and decided that if we did anything, nobody should have to quit school to do it. For my part, I knew that I had to find a job. We decided to stay in touch in case anything new developed. Then they went back to their classes and I went back to Mexico City.

When I got there I found that my brother was making preparations to move to Oaxaca City, where he'd found a job. There were now three of us in the apartment: me, my brother, and a *paisano* named Fabián. After a few days, my brother went to Oaxaca, asking only that Fabián and I take care of the furniture in the apartment, all of which belonged to him.

A week or two later a letter came from Drone saying that in about three weeks there was going to be a congress of representatives of *campesinos,* and that it wasn't a meeting of *Licenciado* Miranda's group. I had found a job in a little machine shop where there wasn't much work, and the boss told me that if I wanted to take off, I could. I decided to attend the congress.

⁓⁓⁓⁓⁓

The meeting was held on an *ejido* called El Zacatal. It lay about a kilometer off of the federal highway, about three hours out of Tuxtepec. The *ejido* consisted of about fifty houses. Only a half-dozen had walls of cement block. The rest were made in the style of the region: walls of strips of thin wood, and roofs of palm. The streets were as flat as a tabletop. Women, children, and adolescents walked; here and there a man rode on horseback. It was Sunday, a day of rest.

Nothing in the town's appearance told us that a congress was being held. There were no banners or signs, as is usual when a *campesino* group holds a big meeting. But people kept coming, men with sun-cured skin and callused hands, some with sandals, some with shoes.

As we were coming into town a graying man in his fifties invited us to take seats in what was called the "meeting room." It was a *pala-*

pa like the others in town, but with a cement floor. A part of one wall, about three meters across and a meter high, was made of cement blocks: that marked the forum. Our seats were desks used by the students and borrowed from the school. The meeting began about noon, nearly two hours behind schedule. About a hundred people were present.

The short, dark, graying man who had invited us to the *palapa* took the floor. He said that his name was Raúl, the director of the Zacatal *ejido*. We elected him president of the gathering. A *campesino* named Idelfonso was chosen to supervise the discussion, and the group chose as secretary the teacher at Zacatal's school.

The first order of business was for each of us to stand and introduce himself, saying where we were from and what group we represented. The four of us said that we were from the Juárez mountains, but did not represent any group. Then we went around again, with a representative of each community telling what problems his people faced. The problems were similar. One by one, each spokesman added to the list of names of hired guns who worked for the landlords, the list of those *compañeros* who were jailed or facing arrest, the list of those who'd been murdered or beaten. There was an endless recitation of the dates on which the communities had appealed to the Ministry of Agrarian Reform for help, with a common result: Nothing was done. A list of functionaries who'd been high-handed was also developed. Someone reported that one of the bureaucrats had told a delegate that, "Yes, we're going to give all of the *campesinos* their little pieces of land—three meters underground." The names of the landlords included that of a former governor of the state of Oaxaca, *Licenciado* Víctor Bravo Ahuja and his family.

The common themes of the *campesinos* were property titles, the recovery of communal lands, and new centers of settlement. For example, one man told the history of the *Ejido* Gustavo Díaz Ordaz in the state of Veracruz.

The Díaz Ordaz *ejido*, its representative told us, had been created by a presidential degree issued in March, 1968. It gave the inhabitants of the *Ejido* Arroyo Denesa permission to expand the *ejido's* limits into land that had been illegally taken by landlords from Playa Vicente, Veracruz. Díaz Ordaz was the president who ordered the massacre of the students in Tlatelolco square in 1968; the *campesinos* had probably named the new settlement after him in hopes that it would speed their petitions and protect them against abuse. But their magic name had been as useful as a widow's cries for the resuscitation of her husband. In May of 1968, one hundred and fifty state policemen, supported by gunmen who worked for the landlords, arrived in trucks that belonged to the landlords and assaulted the settlement during the day, when the men were out working the land. The invaders held the women and children at gunpoint and sacked the place.

They went into the town hall and took away its records, including those that granted the *ejido's* right to exist. They emptied the community's granary of corn and beans and, on top of that, took fifteen thousand pesos from its Society of Parents. They detained a couple that was teaching at its school; neither had been seen or heard from since.

Then they formed a wall to wait for the men to come in from the fields. As the men entered the town, the invaders fell upon them and forced them to knock down their huts—their homes. When that was done, the troops set fire to the rubble and loaded the *ejido's* inhabitants into the trucks. They drove them to the federal highway and left them there. The *campesino* who told of these events had denounced them to the appropriate authorities, but of course, nothing had been done.

Similar stories were told by people from communities named Xochiapa, Lázaro Cárdenas and Ignacio Ramírez.

Other speakers mentioned *Licenciado* José Francisco Miranda, the peasant leader of whom Driver had spoken. The leaders of Xochiapa had gone to him for help in rescuing two *compañeros* from jail in the town of Cosamaloapan; they'd been arrested for resisting an invasion like that at Díaz Ordaz, again, in a settlement protected by a presidential decree. Miranda had demanded seventy-five thousand pesos as a fee for representing them. The cost of filing the necessary documents, the *compañero* told us, was forty-four pesos, plus eighty pesos for official stamps and seals.

Miranda had also come into the region to organize rallies for candidates from the Partido Revolucionario Institucional, or PRI—since 1929, Mexico's ruling party. He'd told the people that by showing their support for the PRI, they could count on more favorable attention from the Agrarian Ministry in the future. At his urging, they'd gone into town for a political rally. Miranda had promised them lodging and food; their lodging was the truck bed on which they rode into town, their food, canned goods. Yet the *campesinos* knew that the PRI was paying him to build the party's rallies.

A young curly-haired man, thin as rail, and another dark-skinned youth introduced themselves as spokesmen for students at the teachers' college in Tuxtepec. The *campesinos* gave them an especially long round of applause, because there weren't many educated men in the hall.

"It gives us a great pleasure to be here," the student leader said, "even though you are trading stories of bitter experiences. But I'm sure that your exchange will allow everybody to go back and continue the struggle with a renewed spirit and strength, knowing that we're not alone or asleep anymore.

"We students at the Regional Center for Normal Teaching are carrying out our own struggle, and we're here with you because we are neither blind nor deaf to the injustice that prevails in the countryside. Our struggle is based on the Mexican Constitution, which says that everybody has a right to an education."

The student said that the teachers' college had set a limit on the number of people who could take its entrance exam. There had practically been an uprising among those who hadn't been permitted to take it, and at last, they'd won the right. Then they had to battle to be allowed to enroll. They'd held marches and demonstrations in the city, and invited into their ranks *campesinos* whose organizations were demanding solutions to rural problems. In response, the authorities had created groups of student reactionaries, who—in view of federal troops—had attacked a demonstration with machetes, sticks and even pistols.

In order to get the entrance exam administered, the students had protested in the capital, with the support of the Oaxaca teachers' college, the Benito Juárez Autonomous University, and the Peasant Independent Front of Oaxaca. The authorities gave in. But when the students got back to Tuxtepec, the school's directors had played a new trick: Classes would begin, they said, only after the expulsion of twenty activists whom they'd identified. The whole student body was offended by this action, and it again organized a march. This time, they were halted by federal troops. The legal means of protest were closed to them.

So they hijacked city and rural buses and official cars—sixteen in all. Their seizures halted bus service to the Papaloapan basin. They were threatening to burn a vehicle if their demands weren't met, when the education authorities came to offer a new agreement. Classes would start, they said, when the students returned the vehicles. But after school started, eight of the activists were arrested, three of whom remained in prison.

"This, in general terms," the student leader said, "is the situation of our movement. *Compañeros, campesinos*, we have to unite forces so that our voice will grow stronger every day."

Strong applause rippled through the hall.

Driver also spoke, telling more or less the same story that he'd told Tío. One of the last to speak was *compañero* Raúl, who told the story of the *ejido* that was hosting the congress. El Zacatal, he said, had been an official population center since 1974. But the land on which it sat was claimed by a man named Joaquín Caraza, who told the authorities that he was a small farmer. The townsmen said he was a big landlord instead. In a meeting before the Public Ministry, he'd been asked to show documents that would back up his claim. He said that he had filed them with an office of the Agrarian Ministry. Then he'd shown other documents that spoke for another piece of land, not the one on which El Zacatal sat. But overnight the Secretary of Agrarian Reform declared that the rightful owner of the land had appeared, and that the people living on the *ejido* had to move away.

The chairman proposed a recess because we'd already been listening for four hours. His proposal was accepted by acclamation. During the break, my friends and I walked through El Zacatal's dirt streets, which were broad enough for two vehicles to pass. By chance we found ourselves at the home of Raúl, the leader of the conference. His house sat on a lot of fifty by fifty meters, the same size as all of the other lots in town. He had surrounded his house with a wooden fence, which was covered with vines. Inside the yard were a banana tree and two young mango trees. His hut looked like the rest, with a shaded entrance on which hung a hammock.

The student leader was resting in the hammock. His companion sat in a crude wooden chair. Raúl, on seeing us, invited us to the porch and produced more hand-made chairs. Then he went inside and brought glasses of lemonade.

We introduced ourselves to the students. The thin one who had made the speech said that his name was Adán. His assistant was named Isidro, but he said that he went by the nickname "El Sandwich," because he was the only person around who could pronounce the word properly, as in English; maybe that was because he was missing two or three of his upper front teeth. He said that he'd lost them during a demonstration when a soldier hit him with the butt of a rifle.

"I have faith," *compañero* Raúl said, picking up the thread of conversation that they'd dropped when we walked up, "that this congress is going to produce an organization whose *campesinos* won't abandon one another."

"You can be sure of that, *compa* Raúl," Adán said, shortening *compañero*.

The chat could have continued but about this time *compañero* Raúl looked at his wristwatch and said that it was time to get back to the meeting.

The secretary reopened it by saying that from the morning's reports, it was clear that the problem of the *campesinos* was the problem of land, enough land to provide a decent standard of living. The obstacles were, first, that the best lands were illegally in the hands of landlords, and that, despite many petitions from the peasants, the authorities had intervened largely on behalf of the landlords. In the few cases where the *campesinos* had won redress, the landlords had sent in their hired guns. When the thugs came to throw people off of the land, they often came with soldiers and police in tow.

He then told the gathering to think about what the congress should accomplish. The meeting couldn't be just a way for getting to know people and trading stories, he said.

Compañero Raúl took the floor. "The way things are right now," he said, "we're in a shameful situation. Just look at who's here at this congress! We are Chinantecs, Zapotecs, and Mixe, the ancestral inhabitants of this land. Our forefathers were the owners of this land. We have our own customs, our own languages; we are the authentic sons of these lands. All we've been asking for are pieces of land inside our own country! Isn't that a bitter irony?

"The teacher has summed up for you the results that we've gotten from asking the agrarian authorities for land. These lands are communal lands, belonging to us. We are the *comuneros.* In 1711, the king of Spain recognized that we are the legitimate owners, and his viceroy gave us titles, referred to as the Primordial or Original Titles. These titles were confirmed in 1856 in a decree that says, 'No property title after 1711 has any validity against the Primordial Titles.' Therefore, *compañeros*, our struggle ought to be for the recovery of our communal lands!"

Every hand in the audience applauded *compañero* Raúl, and some people shouted, "That's right!" or "Bravo!"

When everyone was quiet again, Raúl resumed. "I propose that to carry forward our purposes, we right now form as association of indigenes, an association of *campesinos* for self-defense. I have a name in mind, The Indigenous Association for *Campesino* Self-Defense. If right now we represent fifty or sixty villages, I am sure that before long, we'll be bigger. We've got to grow strong enough to force the government into resolving our problems."

Other *compañeros* rose and supported the points that Raúl had made. Some of them said that we needed more suggestions for a name. One man said that for an organization to grow, it would need a brochure to explain our point of view. But ultimately, the proposal from *compañero* Raúl was accepted, and we proceeded to the election of representatives. Raúl was elected president, and delegates were named for each of the regions that participated in the congress. We named Drone as the representative of the Juárez Mountains, even though there were only the four of us.

As we rode back that night towards Tuxtepec, I thought about the speech by *compañero* Raúl. We were called indigenes because that's what Christopher Columbus—known to every school child—had named us. He thought we were Hindus and also called us Indians. Anyway, the names are of little importance; he charted a course that condemned us forever.

The Spaniards invaded us, subjected us, and robbed us. Our lands were so vast that even now modernity hasn't finished robbing us. But if things continue as they have, someday they'll forbid us to die so that we won't occupy the ground of a burial plot.

Ever since the fall of Tenochtitlán, we, the indigenes, have been the fallen tree, and everybody—Spaniards, mestizos, foreigners—has made firewood of us, generation after generation. They made us take gold out of our mines so that they could rob it. The indigenous *campesino* was the rank and file of Don Miguel Hidalgo y Costilla and of Emiliano Zapata, but we were beaten after a few victories. Our people were also the troops of the oppressors. They had made us kill one another and we had come to a point of being helpless. Today the sociologists call us "the marginalized" and the politicians call us "those who have the least." It's only a continuation of the name-game.

We don't have gold anymore. They've taken it away. They have trampled us so much that we've become almost embedded in the ground. We can't even rise to look in the mirror; they have made us ashamed of our race. Our brothers who have been able to advance themselves have believed that when they begin wearing shoes and parting their hair, they are no longer Indians—and they become capable of taking up their hatchets, cutting us into more firewood.

In the cities, when anybody says *indigene*, everybody thinks of a poor, ignorant, dirty *campesino*, and when anybody makes an error at work, they say, "Don't be such an Indian." But even with all the centuries that have passed, they haven't been able to dispossess us of everything. We still have our customs. We are folklore for the tourists.

When they see an indigenous woman in her embroidered dress, molding the clay for the pots that she'll use, they are amazed. What they don't know is that she lives in misery. The merchants have turned even our customs into commerce: They get rich and we go on living hand-to-mouth.

My friends and I spent a couple of days in Tuxtepec discussing the congress, but we couldn't come to any conclusions about what we should do to help the Association in the Juárez Mountains. So I decided to visit Driver, who had invited us to come to his house whenever it was convenient. He lived in a little settlement about three kilometers outside of Valle Nacional, at a place where the highway ran parallel to the river. To get to his place, it was necessary to cross the river, but there was no bridge. One had to take off one's shoes and pants and wade through it.

It was summer and the current wasn't very strong, but in its deepest part, the water came up to my armpits. When I came out of the river, I found myself on a piece of gray land that looked like it had been through a slicer. Everything had been plowed up. About five hundred meters away was a house of the same color as the soil. Driver, who was lying in a hammock between two trees, recognized me as I walked up. He signaled for me to go into the house.

He had a lot of children. A dark-skinned woman sat in a chair with a fat-legged baby in her arms. Four other children were playing on the ground. Three were shooting marbles, and the fourth, a little girl, was trying to make a plastic doll stand on its feet in the dust. Two of the little boys were barefoot and clad only in T-shirts.

"Moisés," Driver said to one of the boys, "bring us a chair."

"*Vieja*," he said, speaking to his wife, "why don't you make us a lemonade?"

She got up and went towards the door, and the baby whimpered a little, maybe because she had laid him down in a cradle so that she could take care of the chore. She was of medium height and of uncertain age; five children had left their mark on her. She was dressed in a flowered cotton shift that fell down below her knees.

Driver was wearing a cotton shirt and khaki pants.

"What's new, *compañero*?" he asked.

"Nothing in particular. I just decided to stop by," I told him.

Moisés was struggling into the room with a chair that was taller than he was. I went to help him, and he looked up at me without saying anything. I rubbed my hand through his curly hair and, taking the chair from him, told him thanks.

"I appreciate your visit. That's what *compañeros* are for," Driver said. "Whenever you want to come by, my house is yours. It's a very humble place, as you can see, but there will always be somebody here to give you a sincere welcome, a roof over your head, and at least a plate of frijoles with tortillas."

I had to respond to an invitation like that with thanks, more than once. But pretty soon I explained my business to him.

"The problem is that me and my *paisanos* haven't been able to come to any agreement about what we can do to work with the Association," I said.

"The job is to organize, brother," Driver told me.

"Well, that's exactly the problem," I explained. "From right here, from this region to the mountains there is a difference as great as the altitude. Here, you at least have the experience of being organized; the only problem is the leadership. Here, the villages are only a half-hour from each other; there, the walking distance between them is about three hours. Up there, we hardly know the people in the nearest village."

Driver's wife brought out two big glasses of lemonade and returned to the kitchen.

"Well, the important thing is that you guys want to help, and you're young enough. When a person is young, he's full of energy. I'm not old, but I have to worry about my family's survival."

"But the problem," I continued, "is that the adults aren't going to take us seriously. What authorities are going to lend an ear to us? We're just kids without experience. They'll probably give us a scolding."

"If that's the case, I think you all ought to go talk to Tío," he said.

I agreed. After that, we talked about minor things. For example, he told me that the land around his house wasn't all his. It was divided into plots of one hectare each. His pickup, he said, was at a friend's house on the other side of the river.

I said goodbye to the family and went back towards the highway, stopping to swim a bit in the river. When I got back to Tuxtepec, I presented the idea of visiting Tío. The others had classes to attend, and so they decided that I should go alone. Between the four of us we pooled enough money to pay for my trip, which I began three days later.

Having learned from our first experience, this time I had prepared. I'd left early in the morning so that nightfall wouldn't catch me still halfway there, and I carried three sandwiches. A bus carried me as far as the turnoff to El Porvenir. The town stood two kilometers from the road. As I came into it, I noticed that it was quiet, like most of the villages. All I could hear was the sound of *cumbia* music and commercials from a transistor radio somewhere. Further on, I came past the store where we'd had soft drinks on the first trip. I stopped in again. The storekeeper was there just as before, resting with his elbows on the counter. You could have moved him to a wax museum and he wouldn't have known.

After I twice yelled out "good morning" in the young *campesino's* yar´, the old man who had received us on the first trip appeared.

"Come on in, *compañero.* What can we do for you?" he asked.

"Nothing, nothing," I said. "I'm going to Paso del Toro to see Tío and I just thought I'd say hello."

"Oh, I can see that you don't know," he said, with a seriousness that bode bad news. "There was a problem between the *campesinos* and the landlords and a column of police went to take over the village. Tío isn't there anymore. He had to go somewhere else.

"And if I were you," he added, "I wouldn't think of going to Paso del Toro. If the police see you, they're going to want to know why you've come. It seems that they've got an informer who tells them who the *compañeros* are. It was a good idea that you stopped to see us before going on."

"How far away did Tío go?" I asked.

"He's a long way off, but it's easy for you to get there because you can go by bus. He's in a town called Miguel Hidalgo."

He then told me that all I had to do was return to the road and catch the next bus that passed. I said thanks and went back towards the highway.

Tío's move told me that danger was always near. I had felt that fear when I'd talked to him. The security measures around him had inspired my fear. My friends and I had already talked about the danger of getting caught in a raid like the one on Paso del Toro. But we'd assured ourselves that the activity that we foresaw wasn't illegal. We only wanted to teach our *paisanos* about their rights in dealing with the paper company. We didn't see why we should fear doing that.

The bus was an hour or two in coming. It was a small bus, and its roof was covered with bundles. It was full of passengers, too. Those who were sitting looked as if they'd been lashed to their seats while asleep. Those who were standing, hands on the interior luggage rack, looked bored and tired.

At every junction in the road the bus stopped, letting off passengers and their bundles. Every time that new passengers would get on, the driver would look into his rearview mirror and in a nearly mechanical tone say, "To the rear, please. Go on towards the rear. There are seats in back." But it wasn't true. It was so crowded that the ticket collector sometimes had to walk on the backs of the seats to reach the people at the rear. Despite the driver's instructions, I stayed near the front entrance so that I could see the town signs as we passed.

Miguel Hidalgo was a brand new settlement that the highway divided in two. The land that it set on was hilly and uneven. None of its streets were straight. Trails ran among the foliage from house to house. The houses had roofs of palm or tar-paper. The houses were scattered and nothing seemed to mark their property lines. Where there was neither a trail nor a yard, all kinds of foliage had sprung up, dotted by charred tree trunks.

The only concrete building in view was one that looked like a school. It was a rectangular building, divided into two sections. Tires that had been cut in half seemed to be growing in a row on its play-ground. There was also a wooden structure that looked like a gallows, only it had a bell instead of a rope.

The settlement consisted of forty or fifty houses, and that created a new puzzle for me: Where was I to find Tío? The logical course of action was for me to ask, but who would answer questions from a stranger? And if people didn't know who Tío was, wouldn't they think that I was crazy, asking for my uncle? I decided to use what was now becoming a standard procedure: to go to a store, buy a cold drink, watch, wait, and think. But I couldn't see a power line anywhere, some-thing that would tell me where a refrigerator might be. So I asked a little boy who was passing. He was carrying a piece of wood and an unsheathed machete. "Over there," he said, pointing.

The storekeeper, of course, was not to be trusted. If he didn't have a steady stream of customers to keep him busy, I told myself, he would try to find out even what brand of boots I was wearing. The men who tend stores are that way, but I didn't think that the women were the same. They didn't seem to pry, and the younger ones even seemed trustworthy.

The storekeeper was a man; he was accompanied by his wife in the store. I took my drink outside and sat on the trunk of a tree. The drink was a little cooler than the room temperature would have been, but not much. I unrolled my packet of sandwiches, now flattened, and began to eat when I heard a voice behind me.

"Are you selling something, young man?"

It was the storekeeper's wife, a round-faced, dark woman of about thirty-five. So much for my theory that women don't pry, I said to myself.

"Sandwiches, ma'am," I told her, just to say something. "But, since nobody buys them, I'll just have to eat them myself."

I opened my packet and showed her the two sandwiches that remained. It was obvious that I hadn't told her the truth. She smiled a little.

"Pardon the question," she said, "but the thing is, sometimes ven-dors come around with *chiles* and other things that we can sell, and since I'd never seen you around here . . ."

Here's your opportunity, I thought. "This is my second time to visit this town," I told her. "A friend lives here. His name is Güero."

"Güero? Which Güero? Here there are two or three men who are *güeros*," she teased. I had awakened her curiosity, and she was going to follow it like a cat does a mouse.

"This man has a light-skinned daughter with brown hair," I said, indicating the child's height with my hand.

She closed her eyes for a moment, as if trying to remember.

"Ah, a man with a big mustache!" she said.

I nodded my head and, to change the subject, told her that in the hot climate of that town, they needed to keep their soft drinks colder. She said that the village had already asked the Federal Electricity Commission to bring in power, and that when it did, she and her husband would try to buy a refrigerator.

I paid her for the drink and casually asked her which of the trails would take me to the house of the *güero* with the big mustache. I said that I didn't remember very well just how I'd gone on my earlier trip.

"Take the trail that goes up that little hill," she said, pointing to one side.

Everything had turned out as I had hoped. As I came to the top of the hill, I saw Silvia, Tío's wife, at the door of a hut. She was throwing a bucketful of water into the yard.

Silvia raised her hand in greeting. She was wearing a red bandanna on her head in the style of José María Morelos. She waited until I came up and then invited me in. Two huts, joined together, were their new home. The first of the two was a kitchen. Their dishes were the same ones that they'd had at Paso del Toro, the same corn grinder was there, now attached to a new post. In the second hut, about four meters square, was a cat and some wooden benches. The brown-haired girl was asleep on one bench, a blanket beneath her as a mattress, another blanket at her head for a pillow. Everything was the same, except that their floor space was smaller and the roof of the hut lower.

I explained to Silvia how I'd found them. She said that when the police raided Paso del Toro, as usual, the *campesinos* turned out to be the losers. Some were beaten, others jailed. The police were asking questions about the man that they knew as Güero Medrano.

Tío wasn't home when I arrived. He'd gone to work in the fields with some *compañeros* from a neighboring village. On one of the benches I found a set of books with cream-colored covers, and there was nothing to do with my time but leaf through them. They were the works of Chairman Mao.

Not until nearly sundown did Tío come in, with three *campesinos*. All four were carrying machetes, only one of which was sheathed.

"Hello there, *compañero* from Tianguis . . . What is it called?" Güero said to me.

"Macuiltianguis," I corrected him.

"Ah, that's right," he said as we shook hands. "But from now on I'll call you Tianguis because that sounds better. Besides, it means a 'poor peoples' market.'"

The *campesinos* introduced themselves. A delegate from their village had attended the congress, but none of these three had gone, they said. They and Tío decided to meet again that night, and then the three left.

Silvia told us that food was ready, and Tío took a plastic cup of water outside to wash his hands.

"*Compañero* Tianguis," he said when he came back, "let's eat."

Now, besides being a *compañero*, I was also *Compañero* Tianguis. I had been baptized again!

There was no table where we could sit down. We sat on benches. I reheated one of my sandwiches and added it to a glass of lemonade and a plate of black beans.

"What's new, *compañero*?" Tío asked me while we ate.

I told him what I'd explained to Driver.

"Well, what you can do is talk to your *comuneros* and maybe prepare a leaflet that lays out the situation for them," he advised. "That's so that the people can know what your intentions are. They'll either decide that what you say makes sense, or doesn't. They know what they need better than anybody else does. Our job is only to persuade them to do something about it."

Walking through the Zócalo Square in Mexico City, and also in Oaxaca City, I had a thousand times been given leaflets by peasant and union agitators. The agitators usually carried placards listing their demands, and somebody would usually be appealing to the passersby for donations, "Give what you can."

I had always dropped a peso or two into their collection and taken a leaflet, but rarely had I paid attention to what it said. I'd fold up the leaflet and stick it in a pocket, just to keep from littering.

The difference between what Tío proposed and what I'd seen, I realized, was that we weren't to leaflet for money. And we were to leaflet the people who were directly concerned, not the general public.

"But we don't know how to make leaflets," I told Tío.

"When you were born, you didn't know how to talk either," he said. "You'll learn, *compañero*."

A little while later we went outside and sat down on a couple of the tree trunks that were everywhere. Tío sat with his arms around his right knee. I took a pen in hand and laid a notepad on my thigh. We talked again about conditions in the Juárez Mountains and he dictated a leaflet to me, beginning with the words, "To the *compañeros comuneros*." After drafting it once, I made a clean copy.

"A leaflet has to be short and easy to understand," he told me.

"You guys are at least lucky enough to have been to school," he continued. "I went, but only from time to time. I never finished a single year. My family had to go from place to place, working to survive. I was born in the mountains of Guerrero, where even the lizards have to work in order to live. I learned to read from some *compañeros*, but I still can't write very well. You should see my handwriting!"

Maybe he couldn't write, but the leaflet that we had composed seemed nearly perfect to me. We signed it with the name of the Indigenous Association for Campesino Self-Defense.

"The Association needs an organ of information," he said, as if speaking to himself. "Something that will discuss the problems of each village, so that people can see that they're not alone, that they aren't the only ones that face the same problems."

I interrupted him.

"Tío, I'm going to reproduce this leaflet. We'll hand it out in the villages. But what do we do after that?"

"Hand out the leaflets and talk to the people. Tell them that you are the representatives of the Indigenous Association in the mountains. Tell them about what you've seen and heard at the meetings."

"Tío," I asked, "how is it that you're not afraid to live here so close to the highway, when it seems to me that you're always in danger?"

"One must trust the people, *compañero*," he said. "If we don't, how are we going to make a revolution? In a little village like this, there is always an eye open, twenty-four hours a day."

About nightfall a little boy of about nine came up the hill. On his head he carried a basket covered with a cloth. He said something at the door of the house, and Silvia went out to see him. He was the bread vendor.

A little while later Silvia came out with two plastic cups of coffee for me and Tío, and the little brown-haired girl came behind, carrying bread on a plastic plate. Silvia went back inside, got a cup of coffee for herself and joined us. The little girl was sitting in Tío's arms, sipping coffee.

From the hill where we sat we could see smoke coming out of the kitchens of the huts in the village. From each open door came a few rays of light. Every now and then we'd hear the sound of a vehicle on the highway, casting beams on the huts at roadside as it passed.

Five men came up the trail. Three of them were the men that I'd already met. All five carried thin bundles beneath their arms.

"I see we made it here in time for coffee," one of them said, breathing deeply, as if inhaling the vapor from our cups.

Silvia got up to make more coffee, but the *campesino* told her that he was only joking. They'd come from his house and had taken coffee before leaving, he said.

They sat down, one next to the other on one of the bigger tree trunks in the yard. One reached into his shirt and pulled out a package of cigarettes. I'd run out of cigarettes, so I asked him for one. "With pleasure," he said, handing me his package and the matches.

"Now we're ready," Tío said in a casual way.

"Yes, Güero," the one who was smoking said.

There didn't seem to be any hurry. I kept on sipping my coffee and smoking my cigarette. Tío finished his coffee and gave the cup to Silvia. Then he kissed the little girl on the forehead and handed her to her mother.

"Do you want to go with us, Tianguis?" Tío asked me as he was getting up.

"Sure," I said.

⸻

Tío went towards the house and the *campesinos* followed him. I finished my cigarette and gulped the rest of my coffee. Then I helped Silvia take the plates and cups into the kitchen, and joined the group of men.

"Do you know how to fire a gun, Tianguis?" Tío asked. He had two M-1 carbines, one in each hand.

"I've shot at squirrels with a .22, but I've only frightened them," I told him.

I followed him to the kitchen, where the fire gave off light. There he hung one of the rifles over his left shoulder and showed me the other one. He demonstrated how to move the bolt, how to chamber a round, how to put in an ammunition clip and remove it, how to set and release the safety. It seemed pretty simple.

Then he hung the rifle on my shoulder; it was heavier than a .22. Now I was to operate a rifle, not a lathe in a factory. Probably, I told myself, the gun was illegal, even if it wasn't huge.

The *campesinos* were waiting for us when we went back outside. Just as in Paso del Toro, Tío's hut was on the edge of the woods. We took up a trail that only the locals knew. I was the last one in the file. A full moon was overhead, and its faint beams penetrated patches of the overgrowth. I don't know how long we walked. The rifle felt heavy, and I had trouble keeping up with the others.

We crossed a barbed-wire fence, then another, coming into a pasture that had been burned clear. It was so big that I couldn't measure its expanse. It was dotted with burned tree trunks, some still standing, some fallen to the ground. As we passed through the pasture here and there we saw the silhouettes of cows, some of them resting on the ground, their heads raised, chewing their cuds. They watched us pass with the indifference of a king viewing the movements of his subordinates.

The *campesinos* said something and Tío took the M-1 from his shoulder. A cow was about four meters away. On seeing us it moved its head to one side and then another, as if it were trying to figure how to get out of the way. We went on past, then stopped.

One of the *campesinos* took out a flashlight and shined its beam on the cow's head. Then came the dry crack of a single shot. The animal leaped to its right, running. It fell into a little ravine about four meters away.

The *campesinos* went down to where it lay and began talking among themselves.

Tío told me in a low voice that it was possible that the landlord's *pistoleros* weren't far away and might have heard the shot. He pointed to a spot a few meters away, where he said that I should position myself to watch.

I went to the spot that he'd indicated. My hands were sweating. I took the safety catch off the rifle and kneeled behind a tree trunk because I'd seen Western movies and I knew that people always took cover behind something. I scanned the terrain in front of me and saw only foliage swaying lightly in the wind. Nothing suspicious. I turned and looked at Tío, who was about twenty meters away. He had sat down on a big rock and was keeping watch in the other direction. The animal and the *campesinos* were between us.

The moon shone like a big silver coin, surrounded by a misty halo. The scene was quiet, silent. Ten, fifteen, twenty minutes passed.

One of the *campesinos* came up from the ravine with a big bundle on his shoulder. A few minutes later, up came another with a similar bundle, and pretty soon, all of them were out and walking back towards the village. Tío took a look backwards at the pasture, and then he and I brought up the rear. The air smelled like raw meat. The *campesinos* were carrying heavy loads, but nothing slowed their pace. They didn't stop until we were back at Miguel Hidalgo.

When we got back, without putting down their loads, the *campesinos* said goodbye to Tío and disappeared onto the trails.

The only thing that Tío said was, "When the landlords steal the lands of the *campesinos* for pastures, it's only fair that the products of the land belong to the *campesinos*."

By noon the next day the committee had distributed the meat among the villagers. For several days beef was on the plates of the families of the *campesinos* as well as rice and beans.

There was even enough for a barbecue. Three *campesinos* dug a big hole about fifty meters from Tío's hut. The hole was about a meter deep and a meter-and-a-half wide. They covered its bottom with rocks, threw firewood on top and lit it. The fire lasted until the rocks glowed red. They took out the charcoal that they'd made, and then lowered three buckets of seasoned meat into the hole. Then they covered the hole, first with banana stalks, then with banana leaves. On top of all of that they shoveled dirt, so that the heat would be sealed inside. Only a little smoke leaked out. Hours later, there was a great banquet. Everybody got a glass of broth, plus tacos with a sauce that Silvia prepared.

The day after the barbecue, I went back to Tuxtepec with the text of the leaflet. We only had to organize ourselves. Beodo and Drone went looking for Adán and Sandwich from the teachers' college, who promised to provide the paper and to use the school's mimeograph machine to produce the leaflets we needed.

Then the four of us flipped coins to determine who would go to each village. We pooled our money and on Saturday set out to do our work.

My village lies on the edge of the Zapotec district of the Juárez Mountains, next to a Chinantec region. The Zapotec district runs from the coast up into the mountains, and the dialect varies along the way. Those who live on the edges of the district can no longer understand each other's speech, and even in the mountains there are small differences. We can guess what village someone comes from by the intonation of his voice and by some differences in pronunciation. For example, what my village calls *"eta"*—a tortilla—is in other places *"yeta"* or *"gueta."*

Even though I was from the region, the only neighboring village that I'd ever visited was Analco, about three hours away. I'd gone there when our village orchestra had been contracted to play on Analco's saint's day. Beodo, Drone, and Circus Man had also made the trip, and we'd missed our ride home because Beodo had looked up an aunt that he'd never met and she'd prepared a big feast for us.

The flip of a coin determined that I would go to the village of Atepec that weekend. The walk to the village from the federal highway was about four hours long. It was two o'clock in the afternoon before I arrived there. Like most of those in the region, its houses had walls of adobe about thirty centimeters thick, with narrow windows and low roofs covered with metal sheets.

I had brought with me only my jean jacket and a package of leaflets. I went up to the first house that I came to. A Catholic, before embarking on a job like mine, would have crossed himself; a Protestant would have prayed for the Lord to guide his path. I took a couple of deep breaths.

I shouted "good afternoon" to announce my presence, and was greeted by white teeth between dark lips. If what I saw was an attempt at a smile, it didn't work. It was the household dog, its feet firmly planted in my path. I understood that I should stay where I stood and that if I behaved well, it would go running off to give my message to its masters.

A woman in a stained apron came out. Her black hair was in braids.

"Peanut!" she yelled at the dog.

Peanut turned around and scurried beneath her apron.

As I walked across the yard, I said hello to the woman and told her that I was distributing a leaflet that I'd like for her to read. When I gave her the leaflet, all she said was, "Ah."

"And your husband?" I asked.

"He's out working in the fields," she said, turning her eyes to the leaflet without seemingly to read it.

I told her that I'd come back again to talk to her husband about what the leaflet said. "Ah," she said again.

That was it. I went back towards the road. The dog went with me, now without making a sound, smelling my boots as he ran by my side. When we came to the edge of the lot, Peanut sat down on his haunches. Peanut was a good watchman.

I went from house to house handing out the leaflets. Not until I'd been to about ten did I find a *campesino* who was at home. He was a medium-size man in his sixties, gray and balding, with a little bit of goatee on his chin. His name was Elpidio.

I gave him the leaflet and talked to him about the Association. Three times he looked from the leaflet to my face, as if comparing them—as if the leaflet bore my likeness instead of words. He didn't make any comment about what the leaflet said. Instead, he asked me where I came from. When I told him, he recited a list of people he knew in my town, asking if I knew them as well. My answers were my passport, because the old man, seeing that I wasn't lying, went inside his house and brought out a couple of chairs. He had folded up the leaflet and stuck it into his shirt pocket. He told me about the various times that he'd visited my village, even about one trip he made as a young man, trying to win the heart of one of my *paisanas*. He said that he had children who lived in Oaxaca City and Mexico City, and that he had once been a bracero in the United States.

"And here in the village, are things good?" I asked when I finally got the opportunity. He'd talked for a great while.

"No!" he said in a discouraging tone. "The village is worse off every day. It's completely lifeless. You've seen the streets. There's no maintenance, and the runoff from rains have made valleys in them. The people are divided into two camps and they can't agree about anything. Now nobody does his part in the festival. The Catholics are one side and the Jehovah's Witnesses on the other. Used to, we were all Catholic and everybody lived in harmony, worked in harmony. Then one day a couple of gringos made friends with a couple of the villagers, and before long, the gringos were coming back with films about the Bible. They showed them in the houses of their friends. Little by little, they got more and more people together, and pretty soon we could hear them singing hymns in their houses. Around here, we call them 'the brothers' because that's what they call each other. I'd have been happy if it was just a difference in religion, but pretty soon they began calling the Catholics 'children of the false religion.' They quit taking part in the festivals, and then they quit going to the town meetings. Their daughters don't go to the dances; their pastime is praying. They say that our entertainment is the work of the Devil, and during our religious festivals they don't step outside of their doors. At school, their children won't salute the flag or sing the national anthem."

He passed his hand over his bald spot as casually as turning a page in a book, and continued. "I say, if a man works, he's also got a right to enjoy himself a little, just as he has a right to eat and to rest. Festivals, for adults, are like recess is for children at school. It's so that you can clear your mind and go back to learning. Life is hard enough without taking away our festivals."

"And what can you tell me about the paper company?" I asked.

"Ahh! The paper company!" Elpidio exclaimed, stressing every syllable. "They're a rapacious, sneaky, bunch of traitors. They're so greedy that Judas was nothing by comparison!"

Then he told me about what had happened five years before, when the mountain villages had gone on strike.

"Do you think that we can strike again?" I asked him.

He stared hard at me, and then a look of incredulity came over his face. Then he scrutinized me more, with an inquisitive and accusatory look. Finally, he seemed to take a sardonic attitude. I imagined him reaching into his pocket, giving me a coin and then patting me on the shoulder, saying, "Here, boy, go buy yourself a piece of hard candy."

"We, the members of the Indigenous Association of *Campesino* Self-Defense—" I began, trying to make him understand. But I didn't continue. I had the impression that he'd glanced at the leaflet and had seen something that he didn't like. That's why, I figured, he'd begun to talk of other things.

"During the strike against the paper company," he said, as if recalling something painful, "Macuiltianguis was the town that agitated for everything. I think that we lost more than we gained, and if Macuil wants to start up a strike again, well, why even mention it?"

I explained that it wasn't Macuil that had sent me.

"Well, in any case," he said, "this is a delicate question that should be resolved only by our officials and the general assembly, not by any association, no matter where it comes from. I'd advise you not to get into something deep. Leave these things for the adults. And please excuse me, but I think that we've chatted quite enough. I've got to go look at some animals of mine before the sun sets."

We said so-long. He went to his pasture, and I went back to my task. The enthusiasm with which I'd begun was fading, and if things kept on this way, I'd be dragging my way out of town in the dust.

I had no better luck at another house. Its residents, a wife, a husband and three children, took me for a salesman. They crowded around the door, the children jostling for space so that they could see me well. Then, on finding out who I was, the father gave an order and the wife and children went back inside. The *campesino* took the leaflet without saying anything. I told him about our association, but his attitude didn't change. He wasn't about to talk. I said goodbye and went on my way.

The sun was about to set and I hadn't covered even half of the town. Right before nightfall I came into the center of town, where I found the school, a basketball court, the church—with big black stains where the rain ran off—and a building with a big sign that said, "City Hall." Not knowing what to do with myself, I stood watching a couple of guys playing basketball. They'd worked up a sweat and pretty soon they quit. One of them put the ball under an arm and they went off.

Meanwhile, I'd made up my mind. There was nothing to do but to introduce myself to the local authorities and to ask for a place to stay for the night. The city hall was built of adobe, just like the houses, only it was bigger and had benches outside.

A man was sitting on one of the benches with his head leaned back against the wall. A palm sombrero covered his face; only his beardless chin stuck out. His hands were in the pockets of a brown jacket, zipped to his neck. His legs stuck out in front of the bench, his feet crossed. He wore black boots with laces.

It had gotten chilly, but he was sleeping so soundly that he snored. Nobody else was outside, and I supposed that he was a guard. A thin ray of light came from beneath the building's door, which was closed. But I could hear voices from inside. I decided to wait. I sat down on a bench next to the guard.

After a while a pack of dogs got into a fight a few meters away, and, making a sound like someone who is drowning, the guard woke up. He turned toward me, adjusted his sombrero, put his hands back into his pockets and was about to go to sleep again when he noticed my presence. He pushed his sombrero back, rubbed his hands in his face, and looked at me inquisitively.

Deciding that he didn't know me, he said, "What's the word? What's happening?"

"Nothing," I said, hoping that the door would open soon.

"Who are you looking for?" he asked, tensing himself, as if ready to work.

"I want to talk with the authorities," I said.

"On whose behalf?" he asked.

"I'm just want to meet them. They don't know me, but I want to talk to them."

"I'll go see," he said.

He got up and went in the door. It was five minutes before he emerged again. He said that I could go inside.

The room behind the door was big, but without many furnishings. In one corner was a glass case for the Mexican flag, and in another case, gold-colored basketball trophies of different sizes. There was a file cabinet standing behind a varnished desk at which two men were sitting. One of them was a thin man in his forties: the mayor, I figured, judging by his place at the center of the desk. Next to him was a younger man with his hair combed back, a stack of files at his elbow: the city secretary, it seemed. There were benches around the walls of the room.

Nobody invited me to sit down, nor was there a chair in front of the desk. I stood in the center of the room while the mayor stared at me and the secretary looked on with indifference. I felt like an accused man standing before a judge who is going to impose a sentence.

"What can we do for you?" the mayor said in a tone courteous but not friendly. He leaned forward slightly, as if ready to listen.

I told him my name and said that I was from Macuil, hoping that the mention of my hometown would ease things a little. The secretary laid down his pen and looked up at me.

I said that I was one of the Association's representatives in the mountains, and that we wanted to inform the citizens about their rights. I also repeated, almost textbook-fashion, what Elpidio had said about the paper company.

Even though I had more or less rehearsed what I would say, I wasn't eloquent and my timidity didn't help any. But I felt encouraged when I saw that they were listening, as if considering a decision of some kind. The guard had even come inside and taken a seat on a bench by the desk.

When I ran out of things to say about our pine forests, I told them about how and why the *campesinos* were organizing in the Tuxtepec area. They let me go on speaking, and when I finished, I gave each of them a leaflet. All three started reading it.

"It's a very good idea," the mayor said. "We need somebody to open our people's eyes."

The secretary and the guard nodded.

I asked them if they had any objection to me distributing the leaflets in town.

"You can do that," the mayor said. "There's no harm."

"Well, that's what I came to ask you," I said, thinking the interview was over. "I want to thank you for your time."

I shook hands with each of them, turned and headed for the door, when I remembered that I'd come to ask for something else.

"Pardon me," I said, "but can you help me find a place to stay for the night?"

They looked at each other without speaking. Then the mayor said that there wasn't any place that I could stay.

The night would be chilly and the early morning hours, worse. I remembered that Tío had told me that, "Like Chairman Mao says, 'We have to rely on the people.'" But here, the people weren't supporting me.

"Well, thanks anyway," I said. "I'll see what I can find."

I was going out of the door when the mayor called after me. He said that they could provide me with a *petate*, a mat. I told him thanks. It was better than nothing.

The guard went to a storeroom and brought out a rolled *petate*. I put it under my arm and told the guard that I wanted to go out for a walk. I paced the streets for awhile, but there was nothing to see. Every now and then I'd come across someone who would say, "Good evening," and then pass on by. After about an hour I went back to the city hall. It was silent and dark, closed. Nobody was there. About twenty meters away stood an oak tree, and beneath it, the remains of a fire that was still smoking. It didn't seem to be on private property and so I went over, gathered some sticks that were lying about and sacrificing five of my leaflets, got the fire going again. There was a stump lying nearby. I pulled it near the fire and sat down.

An hour passed, then two, three, maybe four. The heat from the fire got weaker and weaker as the sticks were consumed. My back was tired and chilled. It was getting colder as the night deepened. When I saw that the fire was giving off its last sparks, I got up and went to the porch of the city hall, laid down and curled into my jacket and the petate. But my coverings were just an envelope for the chill. I tried out something that I'd heard about: that if you keep your body completely still for fifteen minutes, sleep will overtake you. It didn't work. I looked into the sky, hoping that the sun would emerge, but saw only stars twinkling in the blackness of the universe. Noting that my underside was less cold, I shifted and shifted. About sunup I must have had a dream about two seconds long. I dreamed that I was coming into my town on a warm and sunny day, that I had a blanket beneath my arm . . . and that I was cold nonetheless.

"Why do you feel so cold when there's so much sunshine?" I asked myself.

The answer came immediately, because I woke up.

I might have frozen to death if I hadn't gotten up and paced along the porch, doing exercises and jogging in place, meanwhile repeating, sometimes in a speaking voice, "Chairman Mao says that we have to rely on the people." Nothing could have been more ironic. I had gone to the leaders of the people they'd offered me a *petate*. But I was learning. On the next trip, I swore, I'd bring a bedroll.

When the sun came up over the mountains, my mind was dull, but I was at least awake. My eyes were swollen and tired, but my body was warmer. I watched as several girls passed by, carrying buckets of corn. They were going to the corn mill, whose motor I could hear in the distance. After a while men in hats and jackets came out, carrying machetes, on their way to the fields.

I waited while the sun climbed in the sky, then went to a faucet and washed my face in its cold water. About ten o'clock I picked up my packet of leaflets and resumed my rounds.

In some houses nobody was home, but I left leaflets anyway. About noon I came to the mayor's house.

"Boy, you're still in town?" he asked with a little disbelief.

"Well, I haven't gone to all of the houses," I said.

"Where did you spend the night? You must have a car, no?"

"No, they haven't finished assembling my car," I replied. "And I took a hotel room for the night."

His little eyes grew big. He was obviously surprised.

"Don't tell me that you spent the night outdoors."

"There was no place else."

We were about five meters apart: me, in the street; he was sitting in a chair in his yard, sanding a piece of oak that he used as a handle on a hatchet. He shook his head from side to side. "And I'd understood that you had transportation," he said, as if to himself. "The people who come to sell something or to represent some group usually have their own vehicles, so that they don't risk spending the night in a town where they don't know anybody. Your group doesn't give you transportation?"

"We don't have money for buying our own cars. Nobody pays us for distributing the leaflets. I'm even asking myself why I'm doing it, but the fact is, I'm here."

The mayor shook his head again.

"Come on in," he said, all of a sudden, offering me the bench on which he was sanding.

"Sofia!" he shouted from his seat. "Heat up the beans."

I didn't hear any acknowledgment from inside the house.

"You've even got bags under your eyes," he said after looking me over.

"I don't feel so bad," I told him. "It's as if I'd spent the night out drinking."

The mayor smiled for the first time, but it was a little smile. A little while later a woman's voice called from inside the house, saying, "You can come in now."

I followed him into the house and into its big kitchen. A big clay pot was hanging over its fire, and his wife was grinding corn on a *metate* of black stone. On the walls hung clay pots grouped by size. There was a table of unfinished wood in the center of the kitchen. We sat down and I ate voraciously.

When I finished, I told them thanks and asked that they forgive me for not being able to pay for the meal.

"Don't worry about it. Food is sacred and nobody should be denied it," the mayor said.

As I was saying goodbye, the mayor broke in. "Don't forget, young man, that the next time you come to town, this house is your house."

When I went back on my rounds, I couldn't help but think of what Tío had told me: "Chairman Mao says that we have to rely on the people."

Two hours later I finished leafleting and headed back for the highway. I had decided to visit my parents.

That night, back in their house, I went into a deep sleep on my cot. The warmth beneath the blankets made me forget about the night before, even about the long walk into Atepec. The world could have come to an end and that night I wouldn't have noticed.

It was one o'clock in the afternoon before I awoke. My father was out in the fields at work. My mother called me to the table when she saw that I was awake, and my grandmother joined us. She was a short woman with a thin face, a narrow nose, and salt-and-pepper hair. Grandmother was the person who was the most excited when any of her children came home.

That night father joined us at supper. As far as he knew, I was still living in Mexico City. He didn't ask me anything until after we'd eaten.

"So, son, you haven't told us anything," he said, leaning back in his chair, crossing his arms and looking at me.

My mother, who was removing the plates from the table, shot me a furtive glance. She took the plates to the sink and then let me know that she was worried by looking back at me again.

I didn't know how to tell them about my activity, because I knew beforehand that they wouldn't be pleased. For them, good news would have been that I had found a job.

"I've filled out a lot of applications and they've said that they'd let me know when there's an opening," I said.

I wasn't entirely lying. Fabían had promised to get in touch if there were any offers. But I'd already decided to tell them what I was doing while waiting for a job. I went to my bed to get a leaflet, but something in my father's look told me that he already knew. Then it occurred to me: of course he knew! Drone had distributed the leaflets in our town. I went back to the kitchen with the leaflet in my hand, anyway. I gave it to my dad with the look of a little boy who has been caught in some mischief and is waiting a reprimand.

My father glanced at the leaflet and then laid it on the table, shaking his head. "I don't like what you all are trying to do," he reproached. "Where are you leaving your studies? This isn't going to help you. We, your parents, have gone to great lengths so that you can get some schooling. You should study, so that you don't wind up like us, who didn't have the chance. My own father, instead of sending me to school, took me to work. He took me with him, carrying big bundles of merchandise to sell in the villages. There wasn't any schooling. He said that there was no sense in it, that people died the same, whether they went to school or not. I would have liked to have had the opportunity that you have, but now that you've got it, you don't appreciate it. Schooling is so that you can have a better way of life, so that you can progress, so that you can work for a living—not so that you can get into trouble. Who is going to pay you all for this? Yesterday you came in tired, with bags under your eyes, and from the way you ate, we figured out that you'd been hungry wherever you came from.

"Think of your mother," my father continued. "Your mother, who is always worried about you so far away. Every time that we sit down at the table, she worries about whether you have enough to eat. You are mistaken, completely mistaken, boy. Don't think that I don't know how long you've been involved in these things. We already knew that you weren't in Mexico City. We've talked it over with Beodo's dad and Drone's dad. You are just kids without experience. How can you think that anybody will follow you? I know that young people are impulsive, but you'd better put your mind on working. What you all are trying to do doesn't have a point. We *comuneros* already know what a strike is, and nobody that I know is ready to repeat such a thing. If anything were to happen, in any case, it would be the village authorities, and not a bunch of kids like you, who would settle it. So don't waste your time. Time is something that can't be replaced. Think it over. You're old enough to understand what I'm telling you."

When he finished speaking, he turned his chair away from the table and left the kitchen. He didn't ask or wait for any explanation from me. He'd said what he had to say, and that was the end of it.

My mother was still finishing the dishes. I leaned back in my chair, elbows out, hands folded behind my head.

"Understand what your father says, son," she said. "It's for your own good."

When I looked towards her, I saw tears rolling down her cheeks. I got up, went and embraced her, and told her not to worry. I also promised her that I'd stay a while with them.

That afternoon, Circus Man came by the house. It had been his task to go to San Juan Luvina, three-quarters of an hour's walking distance from our village. The town wasn't big, and he'd done his work in a day. All he told me was that everyone had treated him well, the people as well as the authorities. The authorities had even told him that he could call a general assembly, if he wanted. He'd told them that he'd be back.

That night Circus Man and I went to the center of our village, where we met up with Beodo and Drone under the old ash tree.

Beodo had gone to the community of Santiago Comaltepec, which also wasn't far away. But he hadn't had as much luck as Circus Man. They had received his leaflets graciously, but without any result, good or ill. Drone had gone to another outlying village, but its inhabitants hadn't taken him seriously. They'd said things like, "Shouldn't you be doing your homework?" and "Does your father know what you're saying?"

The mildest response that he'd gotten came from those who told him that we should follow the example of Isaías, who had studied in Mexico City and come back with a degree in sociology. From what we knew of him, he'd once been a member of the Communist Party, but had switched to the PARM (Partido Auténtico de la Revolución Mexicana), and then to the PRI. Once somebody had asked him to explain his shift, and he'd said, "Because, friends, I finally figured out that you've got to take the bull by the horns. I've joined the PRI because I want to be a candidate for the legislature. When I get up there, then I'll have ways to help our people."

Drone had nearly gotten flogged in our village. Only Don Carlitos had welcomed the leaflets.

"There's no doubt that nobody is a prophet in his hometown," Drone concluded.

Drone and Beodo, like me, had also been scolded by their fathers. Only Circus Man got off—his father was dead.

Considering everything, our effort hadn't brought much success. The three others decided to go back to Tuxtepec. I decided to remain in the village for a while.

In a few days I learned that the paper company, if not the people, was interested in our work. Our leaflets had gone out to several villages, and had been distributed door-to-door in some. The paper company learned of it, and began an investigation. Its agents determined that the leaflet's authors came from Macuiltianguis and, thinking that only an intellectual could have composed a bulletin like that, had questioned Isaías. He knew who we were, but he didn't tell the snoops.

One morning while I was home I heard the mayor announcing a general meeting, called to hear the PRI's candidate for the state governorship. The announcement came about eleven o'clock in the morning. The meeting was set for noon.

The mayor didn't insist that people attend. He issued an invitation, nothing more. There was no pressure because one party or another was involved, because our village stayed out of partisan affairs. We had no PRI or PAN clubs, nothing like that. The parties had nothing to do with local offices like the mayor's, because those were filled in rotation.

Of course, everyone went to vote in presidential and state elections because the polls were sent from Oaxaca City and voting was a civic duty. Everybody voted, but nobody lost any sleep wondering who might have won.

Candidates had come and gone, officeholders, too, and while they might have made some changes in the cities, in our village life stayed on its usual course. The villagers forgot the candidates perhaps even before the candidates forgot the villagers.

Everybody knew that the PRI always won, and even if people asked what the point of voting was, their questions were just idle commentary. Nobody got excited about any of the parties, nobody campaigned for anyone. People just marked their ballots and went on about living.

Once after an election, I had asked my father for whom he'd voted.

"Well, for PAN (Partido Acción Nacional)."

"And why?" I'd asked.

"Well, because it says PAN," he'd told me, meaning *bread*. "I know that we're always going to need bread."

Fifteen minutes after the call to the meeting, the sound system barked again. The voice it carried was not that of the mayor. Instead, it was the voice of someone whose job in life was to talk. He pronounced each of his words as if it had great importance. He talked slowly, as if waiting for his words to sink in. The voice announced that the PRI's gubernatorial candidate was on his way.

Referring to the candidate, he said: "He is the ideal man, the man that the state of Oaxaca needs, a man with a wide revolutionary background and vast experience, our candidate, Manuel Zárate Aquino."

I don't know if it was from curiosity or merely to break the monotony of village life, but I went to the meeting.

An esplanade about fifty meters long had been laid out between the center of the village and the place where the dirt road from the highway came into town. The village's telephone booth, the jail, the CONASUPO store, the post office, the city hall, a basketball court, and the parish church all lay along that stretch of road. In front of the CONASUPO store, the welcoming committee had placed a large round table with a white tablecloth, on which a microphone sat. To one side the members of the village orchestra were seated. Counting children, about 150 people had gathered. The candidate planned to eat in our town, and for that purpose, his advance team had given the mayor enough money to serve food to everyone who came.

All of the sudden the announcer, a short man with a military haircut, turned on the microphone again.

"He's arriving!" he said, interrupting several conversations.

Instinctively the people looked towards the dirt road, upon which, in a cloud of dust, a series of vehicles were traveling. As if stricken with an attack of hysteria, the announcer once again began extolling the candidate.

"Here comes the candidate of the majority!" he shouted.

One behind the other, the vehicles in the convoy stopped, all on one side of the esplanade. There were five vehicles, plus two that had arrived earlier; one of the new arrivals had windows of smoked glass. Men dressed in suits got out of the vehicles and formed a kind of barricade around the one with the smoked windows. One of the men opened a door of that vehicle, and stood there, half-bowing, as if he expected Miss Universe to step down.

We all knew that the candidate would come out of that door. The announcer was telling us as much, giving emphasis to his words, "Right before your eyes, the candidate of the people! Manuel Zárate Aquino!"

The candidate finally got out. He was of medium stature, with a dark bronze skin and straight black hair, combed back. He wore a white guayabera and dark lenses, and his belly gave the impression that he was used to eating well and taking a siesta afterwards. He seemed to be about forty years old.

He raised his arms into the air and smiled, and the band started playing, just about the instant that the applause began. The candidate walked over to the middle of the esplanade, where the mayor met him, and then the two went over to the podium. Following the mayor was his secretary; following the candidate, a man with a thick black mustache. The men who had gotten out of the vehicles had gone to the sides of the streets to urge people to gather in front of the table where the microphone stood.

The announcer gave the microphone to the mayor, who, in the name of our people, welcomed the candidate to town, saying that we appreciated his visit. This was followed by a musical number from our band, and then by remarks from the man with the thick mustache, who talked a long time about the PRI and its candidate. When his turn came, the candidate reminded us that, thanks to the PRI, we had a CONA-SUPO store, where commodities could be purchased cheaply; thanks to the PRI, we had both primary and secondary schools; thanks to the PRI, we had a post office and potable water, as well. The list went on and on, and included thanks to the PRI for the highway and the dirt road that connected our lives to it.

The candidate's speech was intended to be the end of the show, followed only by music from the band, but then Don Carlitos came forward, asking for a chance to speak.

The noonday sun was bearing down, and Don Carlitos was wearing a wide-brimmed, palm sombrero, which he took off when he reached the microphone. He spoke slowly as usual, greeting the candidate and thanking him for his visit.

"I hope that you won't be like the other candidates who've come here, forgetting us after the election," he began. "Our village suffers many deprivations, and if it's true that we now have some public services, with all due respect to you," he continued, looking towards the candidate, "I want to make it very clear that we don't have them because of the PRI. We have the schools, but we've built them ourselves, with money raised through our festivals, and the same is true of the post office. The water system we built ourselves, and we paid for the materials ourselves; the government didn't pay anything, we paid it all. That's true as well for the electric system. If you'll go to the village library, you'll find there the records of every purchase and every hour of labor that we villagers contributed. The highway wasn't for us. It was opened because our villages have forests that can be exploited, producing profits, but for the big rich men, not for us. After years of logging, the lumberjacks are as poor as ever, but our forests are thinner and our village is losing population. That's why," he concluded, "I'd suggest that you not kid around with us, saying that the PRI has given us what we have. It all came from our elbow grease."

While Don Carlitos was making his little speech, the candidate sat sullenly staring at him. It was obvious that he'd already mentally dismissed Don Carlitos in his mind as a troublemaker. Maybe he'd seen that the townsmen gathered before him were studying his reactions to what Don Carlitos said. When Don Carlitos had finished, the candidate, a smoldering look on his face, went to the microphone to declare, "What's going on here is that you are a bunch of ingrates. From right now, let me tell you: From *my* government, you can expect *nothing!*"

That said, he gestured to his companions to abandon the place. All of them got back into their vehicles and roared back down the road upon which they'd come. We lost sight of them in the dust.

"And the food?" the mayor said after a minute.

"We can't let it go to waste, can we?" one of the musicians said.

Not long afterwards, Zárate Aquino become governor of the state, but in Oaxaca City, his despotism and incompetence gave rise to great waves of protest for his impeachment. The placards that assailed him carried a message that could have been written in our village: "Manuel Zárate, not here!"

For the next few weekends Drone, El Beodo, and Circus Man came from Tuxtepec and visited the other villages. I went to the hamlets in the Chinantec region. The results were everywhere the same, except in the town of Yolox, whose inhabits were poorer and more receptive. In the center of that town were two stores overflowing with merchandise.

The owner of one of them was a short man who was as round as a globe. His cheeks were so fat that, if you looked at him in profile, they hid his short nose. In that town I also ran into several people who had throat tumors the size of an apple, and others who had lost their sight and had to walk with a guide.

One Friday morning I went to see the *compañeros* in Tuxtepec. We organized ourselves for the weekend's work. On Saturday morning Drone and Beodo would take a bus for the mountains. On Friday night, Circus Man and I took a bus to see Tío.

At one of the stops Jorge, the guy who we had met in Tío's company in Paso del Toro, got on. He was wearing the same wide-brimmed hat. We were sitting in one of the rear seats. He found a seat midway back. He didn't see us and we didn't go to greet him. We watched as he made himself comfortable, took off his hat, placed it on his knees, and leaned his head into the backrest.

Because we were afraid that in the darkness we couldn't recognize the spot where we should get off the bus, we had asked the ticket collector to tell us when we came to the village of Miguel Hidalgo. He'd said that he would, but it didn't seem to us that he was really paying much attention. We stayed awake and alert, but about all we could see, looking forward, was the pavement and stretches of mountains. When we looked out the windows to our sides, all we saw was our own reflection. The darkness outside and the dim illumination inside had transformed the windows into dark mirrors.

An hour or two later, Jorge woke with a start. He stared out the window of the front of the bus, then put his face up against the window to his side, using his hands as a visor. It seemed that he knew where he was. Then he got up from his seat.

"Driver, stop here!" he shouted, scurrying towards the front and pulling his hat onto his head.

Thinking that he might be going to the same place as we were, we took notice. The ticket collector was chatting with the driver and hadn't told us anything. The bus was still moving at a rapid speed when I saw in passing a board tacked onto a charred tree trunk, bearing the crudely lettered words, "Miguel Hidalgo." We jumped up and ran for the door where Jorge stood.

"Getting off!" Jorge repeated in a tense voice, thinking that the driver hadn't heard him.

"We've already gone by," the driver said with indifference.

Jorge's face assumed an expression of incredulity. He turned his head towards us, but if he recognized us, he gave no sign. His eyes were blazing with anger. The driver, it seemed, wasn't going to stop. He hadn't even slowed down. The road was straight and flat and with every second we were further away from Miguel Hidalgo.

"Why don't you stop?" Jorge said with a scowl.

"Because we've already passed it," the driver repeated. "I'll stop at the next crossroad."

The crossroad was about four kilometers away, and catching another bus at that hour of the night was practically impossible. We'd have to walk.

"Well, you're going to stop," Jorge said through his teeth, drawing out his words. "You can take your mother to the next crossroad, but not me, *cabrón*."

As he said this, he reached his hand to his waistband, and yanking his shirttail out, came up with a semi-automatic pistol. It clicked twice as he chambered a cartridge, and then he put the pistol to the driver's neck. The driver, feeling the barrel on his skin, twisted a bit in his seat as he looked up at Jorge, seeing only a scowl and threatening stare. The steering wheel turned beneath the driver's grip and the bus zigzagged two or three times before he brought it back under control. The bus slowed and came to a stop beside the road. The driver pulled a lever and the door opened. The driver was waiting for us to get out.

Circus Man and I would have gotten off, but Jorge was in the way. The ticket collector was pressed up against the windshield, nearly trembling, as if it was he, and not the driver, who was under the gun. The passengers were silent, watching but not moving. The driver, whose fingers were nervously tapping on the ring of the steering wheel, went as still as a statue. For a moment, all that could be heard was the hum of the motor.

"You wouldn't be thinking of leaving us here, in the middle of the road?" Jorge said, still threatening but apparently entertained.

When he said "us," I realized that he had recognized me and Circus Man and that that was why he stood in our way.

"Look, Mr. Driver," Jorge said in the same mean but teasing tone of voice. "I get frightened at night. I don't like the darkness and here in the middle of the mountains, the coyotes could get me. Besides, I've got corns on my feet that would bother me if I had to walk all the way back. So you'd better turn this little bus around and take us back to Miguel Hidalgo."

Jorge pushed the pistol's barrel deeper into the driver's neck. The driver turned the wheel and without saying anything, headed the bus back to Miguel Hidalgo, still under the gun.

When we got there, Jorge made room for Circus Man and me to get by. We got off the bus, and then he began backing off, never turning his stare away from the driver. As he came down, he said to the driver, like a priest scolding a disobedient child, "When are you city people going to learn respect for the *campesinos*?"

Inside the village Jorge whistled at one of the huts, and someone inside whistled in response. He signaled for us to go into a recently built hut, about twenty meters from the one in which Güero and his family were living. Inside, we found blankets and cots. Jorge went to the hut and came back after a few minutes, saying that we'd talk to Tío the next day.

The following day, Tío told us that our visit was well-timed, because he and the leaders of the Association had a project under way that we needed to discuss. But to go over it, we needed to wait a day or two for the arrival of the *compañeros* in charge.

We waited. There was nothing to do but kill time. We watched. All during that Saturday groups of two and three *campesinos* came to see Tío. Each group talked with him a while and then left.

We weren't alone in the hut, which, it turns out, had been constructed especially for Tío's visitors. One of those who was staying there was a guy who practically forced us to listen to the *corrido* "Camelia la Texana" for two hours. He wasn't a guy who wanted to be a musician or who was learning to sing the song. He was a *campesino*, about twenty-three, who had taken a seat on a tree trunk in a corner of the hut. Next to him was a portable record player with one record. Every time the song ended, he'd move the needle back to its start, playing the song again. He seemed to be content, nearly excited.

He had hair so long that it covered his neck, and it would have hidden his nose, except that he was constantly running his hands through it, brushing it away from his face, parting it above his eyebrows. He had a triangular face and bronze skin, a wispy mustache and a goatee, not because he shaped the growth, but because it grew like that. One of his upper incisors was sheathed with gold, and whenever we came near, he smiled, said nothing, and returned to concentrate on the music. Sometimes he sang along with the recording, moving his body in rhythm with the music. The only thing that we heard him say was, "It was easy." He was also chewing gum, and with every movement of his jaw, his temples bulged. He looked like one of those frogs who inflate and deflate their necks when they croak.

His behavior, and the song, which talked about the adventures of a smuggler, led me to conclude that he'd just come back from an important mission that he'd carried out proudly. Of course, this was only my supposition, but what else could have put him in such a celebratory mood? He alone knew, and it wasn't proper to ask *compañeros* what they'd been up to: If they wanted anyone to know, they'd tell. It was the same as with names.

Later we came to learn that the long-haired guy was called Artillery Man. His nickname had come about after he'd accompanied Tío on a trek through the mountains. When Tío had asked him if he were armed, the guy had reached into the pocket of his *guayabera* and pulled out a .22 caliber pistol so small that it fit into the palm of his hand. Tío had broken out laughing and had said, *"Compañero,* you're carrying some real artillery there."

Circus Man and I spent most of the day trying to come to an agreement about some paragraphs in a book containing Mao Tse-Tung's five philosophical theses, a book that we'd found among those lying in the hut. One of its lines said, "In class society, everyone lives as a member of a particular class and every kind of thinking, without exception, is stamped with the brand of a class."

We already knew the terms *working class, capitalist class,* and so forth, because we'd glanced through the program of the Party. But we knew them more because we knew how to read than because we understood what they said. We knew that the working class would take power after a "prolonged war," and we'd learned that to say "the PRI" was the same as to say "the government." We'd also learned that the opposition parties had sold out, that they played the game of politics only to give Mexico an appearance of democracy—an image for foreign consumption. On the other hand, we'd also been told that some of the members of these parties could be trusted to a degree. But that was about all that we knew of revolutionary theory.

"*Compañero,*" Circus Man said after we'd read through the paragraphs from Mao four or five times, "where is the brand of my class? This says that every one of us has the brand of a class. What class do we belong to? My family owns twelve head of livestock. Five cows, two bulls, three steers, a *burra,* and a horse. We also plant three parcels, a half-hectare each. Am I a cattleman? Am I a peasant? I'm a student. What class do students belong to?"

I already knew that Circus Man had a brother in the United States who sent home enough money to allow them to hire someone to do their farm work for them. Even the money that Circus Man spent at school came in dollars. Circus Man had worked in the fields at home, but very rarely had he worked, as they say, sun-to-sun. The family's livestock spent most of the year in the village's communal pastures.

"You're not a peasant," I told Circus Man. "At most we could classify you as the spoiled child of a family of poor peasants. I'll bet that you haven't even got a single callus on your hands."

"I'm about in agreement with you, but you forget that I'm a student," he said.

"Okay, so you're the favorite child of a family of peasants, and you're studying, and when you finish, the most you'll become is a salaried worker."

"I'll overlook your underestimation of my ability," he gibed, "because I know that all you'll become is a salaried worker, and I've got the advantage that I'm still studying, while you've given your books to the moths. But let's get serious here. The point is to figure out what the brand or stamp of our class is, and I think I've got it. We're carrying out a campaign to get our *paisanos* to wake up to what the paper factory is doing to them. That's a brand of our class! We're on the side of the poor. But that's not enough. The paragraph says that our ideas carry a stamp, too. That we like to drink? Is that a stamp? I'm quite sure that it's not only the poor who like to drink, but the rich, too. They just buy liquor that's more expensive than mezcal. That we ride buses while they travel in cars—that's a stamp of one's class, I guess. The clothes we wear, the food we eat, and even the way we talk—all of that's a stamp or brand of our class. We're studying with the hope of finding a better way of surviving. But that's another stamp, too. The rich, why would they want to study? The only reason would be so that they don't lose what they have, or at most, so that they can get more. Look at the injustice of it! We're studying, just so that we can maybe have as much as the rich folks have when they are born."

It was Circus Man's way to think aloud and to stare at the sky while he spoke, getting his ideas in order.

He went on brooding. "For example, the teachers and secretaries at the school, what class do they belong to? Their personalities aren't as rough-hewn as those of the *campesinos*. They dress better, they probably eat better and have better houses. A lot of them come and go in cars. I've thought that maybe when I finish school, I might become a teacher and live like them. But when it comes to that, *you're* already lost," he said, needling me, "because you've quit school."

I didn't answer him because I knew that it was just his way of thinking out loud.

"Well," he continued, "so what class do the teachers belong to? They're not rich, but they're not poor. They work, they earn a salary: They're part of the working class!

"But I imagine that everybody works, in some kind of way. I don't know any capitalists, but I figure that they work, too. It's just that they don't do it for a salary or for wages. Like these books say, they live from the labor of others, but I figure that even that's a form of *work*. So if we go around trying to find out who works, we'll get nowhere. I think it's better if we make a turn, simplify things: There are the rich and the poor. But even here, there are some who are poorer than others of the poor, and some who aren't as poor. All I want is to get at least to the position of the teachers."

"But you've already said that that's another one of the brands of class," I interrupted.

"Yes, becoming one of the least poor among the poor," he said, returning to his thoughts. "I imagine that among the rich there are also the less rich and the more rich. But if that's true, where is the 'middle class'? Is it the middle of the rich or the middle of the poor, or the middle between the rich and the poor? They'd have to be those who aren't too poor, but that aren't so rich, either. They'd be those who aren't from here and aren't from there, who live better than those here without achieving the position of those there. That's the middle class, and that's the end of it, *compañero*."

But he went on.

"I believe that every student who is poor has the idea of finishing his studies so that he can be less poor," he said. "I guess that's a selfish idea that we've got to struggle against if we're for the emancipation of the *comuneros*.

"Listen, *compañero*," he said, as if he'd suddenly recalled an idea that had escaped him. "Do you think you'd be capable of doing what Jorge did with the bus driver? Not just drawing the gun, but the whole way that he handled the situation."

"I couldn't say. Who knows?" I told him.

"I can't say either, but I'd certainly like to be able to do it," he said.

The next day a man of about twenty-four showed up. He was of ordinary height, but so thin that he looked weak. His face was an oval and his curly hair, cut short. He had a city dweller's appearance. When we introduced ourselves, he said that his name was Ernesto.

That afternoon we learned that he knew something about medicine and was a university graduate. We learned that because a woman came to Tío's hut in anguish, desperate, cracking her fingers.

"Güero, Güero!" she called at the door.

Tío wasn't there. Silvia answered, "What's going on, *compañera*?"

"My husband is going to die! A *sorda* bit him out in the field."

A *sorda* is a type of snake plentiful in that region. They grow to about three feet long, and as thick as a forearm. Their bites are fatal.

"Where is he?" Silvia asked, referring to the *campesino.*

"He's in the house. Please help me. I don't know what to do," the woman muttered. Her eyes showed that she'd been crying.

Ernesto jumped up from his seat and asked Silvia for a razor blade. He knew that Tío must have kept blades because, light-skinned as he was, he needed to shave. Silvia dug out a new blade from their belongings and she and Ernesto went running behind the *campesina.*

Circus Man and I, seeing the hut that they went into, went there with the idea that maybe we could help. But when we got there we saw that a whole group of peasants had already gathered.

The snake had bitten the back side of the *campesino's* right hand. He'd kept a cool head and had tied a tourniquet onto his wrist before leaving the field. Ernesto made some cuts in the form of a cross where the bite was, and then made the wounds bleed. In the meantime, he dictated a prescription and asked that somebody go to the nearest town that had a pharmacy. Two hours later, the *campesino* was convalescing, out of the risk of death.

The *sorda* isn't the only poisonous snake that lives in that region. Among others there is one whose bite is still more lethal. They called it the *rabohueso*. It is as thin as a little finger and not more than twenty centimeters long. Half of its body is soft, and the other half, as hard as bone. One of the peasants said he had been bitten by one while he was harvesting. The snake, hidden in an ear of corn, had bitten him on the index finger. The *campesino* didn't waste time thinking about it. Without a pause, he'd gone to the nearest tree, unsheathed his machete, put the bitten finger up against the tree's trunk and with one whack had cut it off. It was his finger or his life.

Before sundown that evening, Tío and *compañero* Raúl, who was called "Zacatal," came into the hut along with Old Man Matías, the leader of Miguel Hidalgo.

Circus Man, Ernesto, and I met with them to talk about the project that Tío had already mentioned. During the meeting we learned that Ernesto would edit a newspaper that would be called *El Comunero*; both Circus Man and I were surprised to learn that Ernesto was an editor as well as a doctor. He showed us the format that he'd designed. The name of the newspaper would occupy the center space of the masthead, whose extremes would carry pictures of Francisco Villa and Emiliano Zapata. At the bottom of the two photos would be a brief profile of the life and work of each hero. The foot of the masthead would carry the words, "Information Organ of the Indigenous Association for Self-Defense."

There wasn't much to discuss. The idea had been proposed by *compañero* Raúl during the congress, and with Tío's help, had taken form afterwards. Circus Man and I were in agreement; a newspaper would give our effort a bigger presence in the mountains.

We agreed to come back in twenty days to pick up printed copies of the first edition. Our immediate job was to produce material for the edition's four tabloid pages. Tío had suggested to us that we should write an article about the loggers in the Sierra Juárez, and so with a notebook and pencil, Circus Man and I sat down on one of the tree trunks that were lying around and began trying to compose. We had all the information with us, but we didn't know how to begin an article. Circus Man thought that we should ask Tío, but by the time that the idea came to him, Tío was busy in a chat with Matías and some other farmworkers. We scratched our heads and chins, looked into the sky, at the horizon, and into the deep growth of the jungle, but not a line came out for our notebook. Ernesto saw our puzzlement and came over to us.

"Already stumped?" he said, sitting down in front of us.

He asked us what we were supposed to write about, and we told him all we knew. Sometimes he interrupted our explanation with a question. When we had finished telling him our story, he dictated an article that Circus Man wrote down. It was easy for Ernesto. He asked Circus Man to read the article back to him. Then he dictated two or three corrections. After making them, Circus Man tore the pages out of the notebook and gave them to Ernesto, who folded them carefully and put them into a pocket. The great problem of composing was solved.

"You'll learn as you go," Ernesto said, and the way in which he said it made us feel like we'd be capable of writing when the new dawn came.

～～～～

On one of their trips into Oaxaca City, Beodo and Drone had met a group of peasants from the Chinantec community of San Pedro Yolox. The families, who had been victimized by the political leaders of Yolox, were practically in exile. Over the weeks we got to know them and five or six other families from the group.

What we learned from them came as an embarrassment. We'd told Tío that among the mountain people there weren't any problems with political bosses, that everything was democratically decided, according to our traditions. But in a village just a walk of four hours away from my own, there existed a feudal system where the *comuneros* lived under capricious despotism. There were three *caciques* who ran the place, among them the owner of a store where I'd gone when I was distributing the leaflets.

The families told us of a series of abuses committed without the least of scruples. Yolox, besides having timber-rich forests, also owned fields at a lower elevation, where coffee was grown. The paper company had twenty years earlier contracted for the village's timber production, but the money had stuck to the hands of the *caciques,* and the majority of the population wasn't even aware that timber rights had to be paid. The coffee growers were forbidden to sell their harvests to anybody but the *caciques*, who paid less than the market price. If a grower sold to another buyer, a set of repressions were used. They could be as mild as a verbal threat and harassment of the family, or as brutal as a beating, jail—or even murder. Nobody interfered because the *caciques* manipulated the authorities.

According to what they told us, the storekeeper-*cacique* that I'd visited in Yolox was the bloodiest and shrewdest of the three. When a grower brought his harvest to the store, the *cacique* would even go outside to meet him, throw his arm over the *campesino's* shoulder, talk about "my beloved *paisano*," and offer him drinks of *aguardiente*, on the house.

After concluding a purchase, he'd reach for the account book where he noted all of the debts that townspeople had made with his store, looking for the name of the seller. Almost everybody owed him, and the debts were incalculable, because he supplied almost all of their needs, from agricultural implements to a simple strap of leather for repairing sandals. Nothing was lacking at the store. Its prices were exorbitant, but the peasants were able to take what they wanted on credit.

If someone didn't pay their debt, *pistoleros* who worked for the *cacique* and were under the command of his two sons made threats. If the threats produced no results, a beating came. If that didn't work, the *cacique* would have the debtor locked into the town's jail until he or his family paid. The *pistoleros* acted with complete impunity. They had killed one man by ambush, and another in a simulated public argument; a third, they'd forced to dig his own grave before they pushed him into it.

The *caciques'* families were not timid about their wealth, either. During the carnival celebrations at one village, when the people disguise themselves for street dances, the son of one of the *caciques* had dressed himself as "Mr. Money." His costume was a plumage of bills, as closely-knit as a bird's feathers.

Two of the exiles that we came to know were brothers who had recently been released from the state penitentiary. They had been accused of one of the murders that the *pistoleros* had committed. Nemesio, 25, and Rosendo, 23, were both athletic young men, cheerful and slim. With their wives, who were also natives of Yolox, they were living in Oaxaca City on a rented lot about fifty meters square, in whose center they had built a rude cement-block house of about ten by fifteen meters, with no divisions inside. Both of the men were working as bricklayer's helpers.

We came to know the parents of the boys, as well. Theirs was a young family; the father wasn't much more than fifty years old, his wife, two or three years younger. They had five children living with them, separated in age by two or three years each. All of the males worked as bricklayer's helpers except the father, who was a welder.

Nemesio and Rosendo took us to meet Melquíadez, a talkative man in his forties who led the "floating population." He had been a store-keeper in San Pedro Yolox until he'd objected to the maneuvers of the *caciques*, who began to hound him. He was beaten so badly during a general assembly that he'd been hospitalized. Then the *caciques*, in a "search" of his store, had destroyed most of his merchandise. He'd decided that it was best to abandon the village, taking his family with him. In Oaxaca City he'd bought a lot and built some rooms on it, then started a new store, like the one that he'd had in Yolox. He wasn't a man who sat on his hands. Not only did he help the incoming refugees with food and finding jobs, he'd also begun a judicial process, asking that the authorities investigate and punish the *caciques* of Yolox. On his trips to and from the courts, he'd met members of the People's Socialist Party (PPS), who'd offered him legal aid. It was their lawyers who'd gotten Rosendo and Nemesio out of prison.

Melquíadez believed that sooner or later his charges before the courts would bring the *caciques* to trial and put them behind bars, and that the "floating population" would be able to return to Yolox and resume their lives in peace. The other refugees put faith in him as a man who knew what he was doing, and at his urging, they attended rallies and public meetings of the PPS.

Drone had told Melquíadez about the Association, but the Yolox leader had said that he didn't think that the refugees needed it because the PPS gave them ample support. Drone hadn't argued the point because we were willing to aid them, and because Melquíadez, it seems, viewed us as an extension of the group that he led. He had been the one who had arranged for us to use the PPS mimeograph machine when we needed to print more leaflets. When Drone, Beodo and I had gone to Oaxaca City to do some printing, my job had been to buy the stencils, cartridges, and paper that we'd need, while the other two stayed with the machine.

As I waited for a city bus to return, I was astonished; my mind didn't believe my eyes. Passing by on the street was Magdalena, one of the girls I'd pursued back in the village before I went to Mexico City. I hadn't seen her in two years, but it wasn't the time so much as something inside of her that had brought a change. She had cut her flowing hair so short that it barely covered her ears. She was wearing tight jeans, not the knee-length skirts of old. Her expression seemed mature, not empty and shy, like before; she was a woman who had come into her own. It was plain to see that the old days of "Mother has to accompany me" were gone.

"Hello!" I nearly shouted at her. "So you're hanging around here, too?"

"Yes, I am," she replied. We didn't shake hands because both of us were carrying things.

"I didn't expect to run into you," I said.

"Well, I'm a teacher now," she said. "I'm waiting on an assignment to one of the schools in the mountains."

"A teacher!" I said, a little perplexed. "Congratulations."

I felt humbled. After all, I was a drop-out.

"We'll have to see what you women can really do," I continued. "If you would have stayed in the village, you'd have never left the kitchen." I pulled off my hat and bowed a little towards her.

"Enough!" she said, obviously amused. "There's not that much to graduating. You just have to enroll, go to class, do the homework, and answer the exam questions."

"Well, if it's that easy," I said, "I should have run into you earlier. Me, I flunked the second-year exam at my school. Maybe I should take a seat among your students."

My response made her fix her eyes on me, as if she was measuring me. I looked intently at her, too. There had been changes but her radiance was the same; her dreamy look and her long eyelashes were unchanged. I felt overcome by an alien force, and found myself shaking my head from side to side.

"Why are you doing that?" she asked.

"Just because I can't get over my surprise," I told her. "You see, you've left behind your long dresses and your long hair, along with your early life. I'm more than sure that if I give you the chance, you're going to talk to me about feminist literature, the rights of women, and so forth. I'll bet that if I invite you for a drink, you're not going to blush. Probably you've got an ashtray on your desk, because you smoke, too. By now, your mother doesn't accompany you to dances. You're independent now."

"Enough, drop it, will you?" she said.

"I will, but only if you'll join me," I replied.

"I'm not looking for companionship," she said. "I'm on my way to the Ministry of Education to file some documents."

"I'll go with you."

"Okay, I'll let you go along, but only because I'm bored," she said.

"You weren't cynical like that before," I told her.

I went with her to drop off the documents and then we went to a cafe where we drank a lemonade. I told her that back in the village, I'd once bet the other guys that I could win her heart. I'd lost the bet, of course.

The city of Oaxaca was under patrol by soldiers. Some made their rounds in vehicles on the streets. Others were posted on the corners of the city's downtown. They weren't stopping and questioning anybody, just watching everybody. A group called the Frente Popular Universitario had painted walls all over town with slogans protesting the city's virtual state of siege, but the troops seemed not to notice.

After we left the cafe, we went for a walk. As we walked through the town square, we came upon a demonstration. The demonstrators unfurled banners over their heads demanding that the election of a rector for the university system be respected. The man elected had been a Dr. Felipe Martínez Soriano. Among the banners that I saw were those of the Student Worker Coalition of the Isthmus, of the teachers' colleges in Tuxtepec, Tamazulapan and Oaxaca City.

As the streams of demonstrators moved down the streets and into the square, their chants echoed against the walls of every building. A leader of one of the groups was calling out letters, "Give me a C,"

"Give me an O," and so forth, which the marchers shouted on cue. The letters spelled out COCEI, for the Coalición Obrera, Campesina y Estudiantil del Istmo, or the Coalition of Isthmus Workers, Farmers, and Students. "What's that?" the leader taunted. "COCEI!" the marchers shouted. "I can't hear you," the leader said. "COCEI!" they screamed. "What do we want?" he continued. "A solution!" they yelled.

Their spirit was contagious. We joined the march and got behind the banner of the Tuxtepec Teachers' College. I was hoping to run into Adán, or maybe Sandwich, but they weren't there.

Magdalena told me that she knew all along that they wouldn't be. "You men think you know everything, but what you don't know is that where you're going, we women are already coming back from."

I told her why I was carrying the mimeograph supplies, and that my friends were waiting for me. She volunteered to accompany me to see them, saying that she had nothing left to do that afternoon.

The guys weren't pleased that I'd kept them waiting, but when they saw Magdalena with me, they said nothing. She offered to type the stencil for us, and we gladly let her because she had more ability as a typist than any of us. Its content didn't startle her. She had already seen the original leaflet in her father's house.

"I don't know what you guys are up to, but it doesn't seem that foolish to me," she said.

When we'd finished the job, I went home with her. It was about eleven o'clock at night. She lived in a small house with an aunt and two cousins, the aunt's sons, who were also studying in the city. Her uncle was in the United States, sending money home.

"What kind of hour is this for you to arrive?" the aunt asked.

"Don't worry about it," Magdalena told her. "I ran into some *paisanos* that I hadn't seen in a while, and we stayed to chat."

Magdalena offered me a cup of coffee, and after I'd finished it, she went with me to the little yard in front of the house.

"Thanks for letting me see you," I said. "It's not every day that one runs into good news."

"Is that true?" she teased.

Seconds later we were in an embrace, and afterwards, we agreed that I'd stop by to see her whenever I was in the city. She didn't know to what town the education ministry would send her, but she promised to get in touch when she learned.

~~~~~~

When I was next in Miguel Hidalgo, the whole town was up in arms and a lot of the people were in mourning. One of the members of the committee that Matías headed had been murdered. A couple of days earlier, a bus had pulled up at Miguel Hidalgo and its door had opened. Out onto weeds at the shoulder of the road had rolled the body of a twenty-four-year-old *campesino*. A single bullet had been shot into his mouth. The shot had gone through his front teeth, leaving a hole there, as if it had been drilled. The young committeeman left a widow and three children.

Old Man Matías couldn't stop cursing with every breath. "Güero, look what they've done to my boy," he cried, grabbing Tío by the forearm.

The Old Man talked of the *campesino* as if he really had been his son, probably because the two of them had made so many trips together, processing their appeals for the restitution of communal property.

Zacatal had come in on the same bus. He said that three *pistoleros* had come aboard, not far from the Miguel Hidalgo stop. As soon as they'd spotted the young man, they'd drawn their guns, forced him to the front of the bus, and killed him there. The only consolation that Old Man Matías got from the story was that, as Zacatal told it, the young man hadn't flinched or begged. He'd gone to his death without a word.

Everybody in Miguel Hidalgo knew who the *pistoleros* were from Zacatal's description. They named the suspects for the authorities and told them where they could be found. They named the employer of the killers, too. But they knew that nothing would happen. All of the legal papers that had been filed about the communal lands seemed to have instead been applications for permission to bury the young man at home.

Ever since the landlords had begun taking their property, the *campesinos* had been going to offices, filing complaints, and getting sealed papers attesting to the registry of their pleas. The authorities had never told them yes or no, but had always left them with a little hope that—if they came back with a new set of papers—something might change.

It was of this that the Old Man always spoke when he went to visit Güero in the afternoons. He complained about his old age and about the nightmares that disturbed his sleep. It had been about two weeks after the murder that Old Man Matías had come to see Tío, saying, "Güero, I've got the answer!"

———≈≈≈≈≈———

I went from Miguel Hidalgo back to Tuxtepec. A day or two later Driver came by the *vecindad* in his old Ford pickup. He brought a note in Güero's handwriting, a scrawl that convinced me that, as his intimates claimed, he'd learned to read and write from the *compañeros*. The note came with some money and an address, saying that one of us should go to Mexico City to look up Ernesto. I made the trip.

It wasn't easy to find Ernesto's place because it was in a neighborhood where all the buildings were of the same height and color, like children of a multiple birth. I had to go from building to building, looking for the right number. Even the people who lived in the development were unable to help me; all they knew was how to come and go from their own apartments. Nobody understood the numbering system, if indeed a system existed.

When I found the right building and apartment, my knock was answered by a young woman who would speak only through the slightly opened door. She looked me over, head to toe, suspiciously.

"I'm looking for Ernesto," I said.

"He's not here," the woman said.

"What time will he be back?"

"I don't know."

"It's important that I talk to him," I pressed.

She only raised her head and rolled her eyes. I imagined that behind the door, she was shrugging her shoulders. I didn't say anything. She continued to stare at me unblinkingly, as if trying to figure out what my intentions were.

"Come back in a week," she said suddenly. "Fifteen days, maybe four days. I don't know."

"I have to pick up a bundle of newspapers," I blurted out.

"Ah," she said, as if my words had given her insight. "He's already taken them."

Then her head popped back behind the door, as if activated by a spring. I heard the key turn back in the lock.

As I went down the stairs, I thought that maybe this was the house of Ernesto's parents, and maybe they weren't in agreement with his activities, just like my parents. It was even possible that "Ernesto" wasn't his real name, and that upon hearing the alias, the woman had put herself on guard. If the house that I'd visited was the house of his parents, the woman could have been his sister; maybe she knew about his doings, and his parents didn't. Or maybe she was his wife, and she wasn't in agreement. But if any of that was true, why had he given Güero that address? Then I realized that I was giving too much importance to the event. The important thing was that the newspapers were already on their way. I could compare notes with Ernesto later.

I took the opportunity to spend a few days with my younger brother, Alfonso, who was living in Mexico City with Fabián, in the old apartment. He was a preparatory school student, and there wasn't any reason to worry that he'd drop his studies, as I had done. He wasn't far from graduation, and he planned to go on to attend the National Autonomous University to study psychology.

My parents sent money to Alfonso on a regular schedule, but it wasn't enough to cover his expenses and he had to scramble to come up with earnings of his own. He sold encyclopedias from door to door on an installment plan. Fabián was a student at the Metropolitan University and worked part-time in a store. Between the two of them, they were able to get by.

When my brother asked if I was in the city to look for work, I told him that I had begun some work that I couldn't abandon midway. I told him that I was working with the *campesinos*.

"Isn't it dangerous?" Fabían had asked.

"Well, it is and it isn't. What we're trying to do is raise the consciousness of the *comuneros* in the mountains. According to the Constitution, that's not illegal. But it can be misinterpreted."

I didn't tell them the whole truth. But I did tell them that we could have trouble with the authorities, and that they might even come to their apartment to look for me. That was when they'd asked me what they should do in the event that the police came.

On the way back to Tuxtepec, I stopped in Oaxaca City to look for Magdalena, but she wasn't there. So I took a bus that would take me through the mountains, and I stopped to say hello to a paternal aunt and her family.

My aunt was combing her hair when she opened the door, her head pressed against her right shoulder.

"Come in," I heard her say.

I stepped inside and sat down on one of the stairs inside the entryway. Without pausing from her task, she turned and fixed her eyes on me. That was when I knew that something was amiss. She wasn't acting like before, when she always invited her nephews to have a lemonade or a cup of coffee, all the while asking about our relatives. Her stare was as sharp as a butcher's knife.

"Just what are you up to?" she spat.

I didn't know how to answer.

"What do you call it, fighting for freedom?"

It was clear to me that I should move on. I said so long, turned and went out. I heard her bolting the door as soon as I stepped outside.

And that was just the beginning.

I stopped by the village. My father didn't waste any time. He repeated his lecture from before. "You can't go on this way . . . You're wasting your time." The parents of the students in Tuxtepec felt the same way, I learned, but since the other guys were still in school, their irritation wasn't as great.

I went back to the road, back to Tuxtepec. No one there had

received any word from Tío. Nothing was known about the newspapers. I decided that it wouldn't be wrong to visit Miguel Hidalgo.

I packed my suitcase with a change of clothes, some leaflets, and a couple of books. It hadn't been long that I'd been carrying books with me. I'd started after Tío had asked me why I wasn't studying. I'm told him that I was bored with it. But he was always studying, reading his volumes of Mao.

"You have to study," he'd said. "I'm not always going to be among you. I'm not eternal, you know."

Instead of picking up one of the books that were always lying around his hut, I'd engaged him in a conversation. I'd asked him what I should study and why, because it seemed to me that the usual program of schools was designed to turn out model citizens, not revolutionaries. He'd told me that it was necessary to study the revolutionary experience of other people to better understand our own environment. Besides, he said, I had to understand that there were thousands of thinkers, philosophers of the revolution, that no matter what I studied, it was necessary to study something.

Tío had never been to school, but life itself had instructed him. "One of the first lessons I learned," he told me, laughing, "was from a blow with a rifle butt in the solar plexus." When he was a boy back in Guerrero, "where even the lizards had to battle for survival"—he always referred to his home state that way—soldiers came to intimidate his father, who had also fought for land. Seeing them gun-whipping his dad, Güero had thrown himself against one of them. But he hadn't even knocked him off-balance. He'd been hanging onto the soldier's waist when from somewhere, the rifle butt struck him, putting him out of combat.

Years later and now fighting in the same cause, the soldiers came after him. They arrested him and questioned him for days. They wanted Tío to tell them where the guerrilla Genaro Vásquez was holed up. For two days and nights they stood him in a hole filled above knee-level with excrement; to faint would have been to submerge. When he was thoroughly exhausted, they took him to a room where they held him upside down and spread his arms and legs in the form of a four-pointed cross. His torturer punched him in the stomach so hard that Güero believed that the man's fist would strike the wall. After each blow, Tío fell to the floor with his limbs close to his body; he must have looked like a chain that's been dropped. Though he was nearly unconscious, he remembered hearing his torturer say to one of the assistants that, "This one can't endure anything. Raise him up again."

"I don't now why I tell you these things," he said to me, all of a sudden. "If I keep on, you might run out on me."

Tío had a bleeding ulcer, but he said that he didn't think that the tortures were its cause. Whenever any of us saw him, we asked him when he was going to get treatment for it, but he always had an excuse for not going to Mexico City to see a doctor about it.

Silvia had a little while earlier had been trying to get Luchita, the little brown-haired girl, to draw in a notebook with crayons. Now she joined the chat.

What she and Tío had to say wasn't as detailed as the stories told by people who love to talk about their lives. Over the months I'd already learned that Güero had gone from his native region to Mexico City with the idea of selling crafts that were produced by the women at home. To make ends meet between weekend selling venues, he'd carted fruit and vegetables from stall to stall in La Merced market. One weekend, selling his crafts at a sidewalk fair, he'd met some radical students. Güero had been enthralled by their revolutionary rhetoric, and they by his stories of peasant resistance. They began teaching him how to read, and months later, arranged for him to visit China.

I learned these facts incidentally, while we were discussing the productivity of the communal lands owned by my village. Güero mentioned that the land could produce more; that in China he'd seen the skirts of arid mountains turned into good land by terracing. Over there, they used human excrement as a fertilizer, and therefore, when people went to the bathroom, they wouldn't say, "I'm going to the bathroom," but instead, "I'm going to make a contribution." They let the excrement age and then carried it with them to the fields in buckets.

The solution didn't seem like one that I could propose to my *paisanos*—at least not with a straight face—but it was interesting to learn that on the other side of the globe, people looked at things in a different way.

Tío's stay in China had been for military and theoretical training; he was there nearly three years. The experience, he said, had elevated his morale so much that upon his return, he'd felt as if he could make revolution by himself. He established a squatter camp in Morelos, just outside of Cuernavaca, trying to establish a base of the support. The settlement was called Colonia Rubén Jaramillo, after a peasant martyr. The effort became so popular that professional people of different specialties came to help the *colonos* set up their homes and services, and at one point, even President Luis Echeverría visited. It was in Rubén Jaramillo that Tío and Silvia met; Silvia was a member of one of the professional brigades.

Before long the Colonia Rubén Jaramillo had its own free schools, clinics, and public services. It even had a community-owned mill for producing corn for tortillas. But then the agents of the government came. They were afraid that Rubén Jaramillo would become a model community, imitated across the country. They offered to give Tío a comfortable life, anywhere outside of Mexico. He refused. They gave the *colonos* legal titles to their lots and then began saying that the *colonia* was a nest of guerrillas. Finally, they assaulted it, killing a brother of Güero in the shoot-out. "That day," Silvia said, "several of us had to literally hold Güero to the floor, because he wanted to go take vengeance himself. If we wouldn't have restrained him, he'd have been among the dead." That night, Tío and his closest followers fled.

Tío's tales were interesting, but we both knew that I had work to do—and he didn't know anything about the whereabouts of Ernesto and the newspapers, either. I spent only a couple of hours with him and then hit the road again. My plan was to leaflet a town or two, then head back to Miguel Hidalgo or Tuxtepec.

———※※※———

I went by Oaxaca City, looking for Magdalena. This time I was lucky. We spent an evening beneath a tree, in the shadows cast by the fading sunlight. When it came time for me to leave, to my surprise she said that she had nothing to do for the next couple of days and would be happy to accompany me wherever I was going. That same evening we boarded a bus for the mountains.

Once our bus left the pavement for the dirt roads, it set up a cloud of dusty air like dirty cotton. The windows of the bus were closed because the night was chilly, but when the bus slowed down, the dust came through cracks anyway. It was nearing midnight when we heard the driver call out Piedra Larga, our destination.

We were the only passengers who got off. We watched as the tail-lights of the bus disappeared, then dusted ourselves off and looked ahead. Everything was dark. There was not a sign of habitation there. We looked to one side, and another, and behind us. Nothing. The darkness in the growth around us was a thick as *mole* sauce. There was no moonlight. We could barely see our hands.

"And now?" Magdalena asked, not knowing that I was asking the same question to myself.

It was so quiet that I could hear her breathing. Where was the town? We waited for our eyes to adjust to the dense darkness, but even then, we could hardly distinguish between the *mole* sauce of our surroundings and the road at our feet. But it seemed that something perpendicular led away from the road. That, I thought, would be a trail to the town.

We started walking slowly, step by step, not trusting the ground beneath us. Gravel crunched beneath our feet, an indication that we were on the right path. Our guide was the difference that we could discern between darkness and blackness. My fear wasn't of the darkness but that of being in unknown territory: if we encountered someone, who would they think that we were? Magdalena walked to my left, our fingers curled together.

"I can't see anything," she murmured, as if afraid that the night would hear.

"We're okay," I assured her.

I was beginning to feel more relaxed, like somebody who has just finished a job at hard labor. I wanted to light a cigarette, but suddenly

I heard a faint noise. It was like the sound of somebody exhaling, emptying their lungs. Magdalena stopped cold. We stood still, holding our breath to hear better.

Now we heard steps along with the heavy breathing. I felt Magdalena tremble and press closer to me. I felt the pulse beating in my temples and my hair stand on end. A thousand things ran through my mind. Turn back? But where, if only darkness lay behind? If somebody was going to rob us, I thought, that wouldn't be too bad. We had nothing of value but the money for bus tickets. Then I thought of what might happen to Magdalena. Who was near? How many were there? What did they want?

I reached into the pocket of my jacket, where I carried a pocket knife. I pulled it out and opened it without dropping Magdalena's hand. It seemed that the snapping open of the knife blade had been heard: A second later, a dark object stepped into our path, not more than three meters in front of us. I stepped forward, knife in one hand, Magdalena's hand in the other. The figure said nothing. It just kept on coming, right toward us—and then right past us. That's when we realized what we were seeing.

"A cow!" Magdalena said loudly, as if to let all of her tension escape.

"A damned cow!" I echoed.

She leaned her head on my shoulder and we laughed a little.

Then we moved forward again. About three hundred meters further in we began to hear the sounds of rushing water. Then we came to a riverbank. In the darkness, we couldn't tell how wide the river was. We walked up and down the bank, about a hundred meters each way, but found no bridge.

"If there's no bridge, then the river probably isn't very deep. Maybe we can cross it on foot," I suggested.

Since she didn't say anything, I assumed that she agreed. I took the bag off of my back and handed it to her, then asked her to jump onto my back, her legs around my waist. She obeyed and we stepped into the current.

Everything would have gone well if I hadn't stepped on a rock and lost my balance, halfway falling into the river. My dip was sufficient to wet us both up to our waists. But we made it across the river and once on the other side, we caught sight of firelight, streaming through a window. We headed towards the light.

Just as in the city there's a street lamp on every corner, in the country there is a dog or two at every house. One of the dogs at the house we spied started barking and there was nothing we could do to advance. Not even throwing rocks at him made him quiet down. Finally, one of his owners came to a doorway. Through the beam of light, we could see a woman.

"Good evening," Magdalena shouted.

The woman hesitated a moment, but the voice of another female must have given her confidence, because she started walking towards us. As she drew near, Magdalena began explaining that we didn't know the village, that we'd come from Oaxaca City, and so forth.

"If you'll give us a place to stay for the night, we'll pay you," she said for good measure.

"My house isn't very big," the woman said. Her voice was that of a woman in her forties. "If you want, you can stay in the shed."

"That'll do fine," Magdalena said. "If we can spend the night under a roof, tomorrow we'll be gone."

We followed the woman to her shed. It was a little hut with walls of unfinished pine, with a roof of cardboard. She offered us firewood, so that we could light a fire and dry off. Then she went to bring *petates* and blankets. She also brought in a couple of cups of coffee.

We built a fire, took off our clothing to dry, rolled out our *petates* and crawled under the blankets. I felt like kissing Magdalena's feet. Without her, we'd have spent the night on the trail.

In the morning we gave the *petates* and blankets to the woman, talked her into accepting a gratuity, and went back to the trail. The village lay about two kilometers away. It was a little settlement strewn across the base of a mountain, with houses of adobe and of cement-block and palm. The only flat part of the town was its central square, about one hundred by one hundred and fifty meters square. On one side we saw a couple of stores; on another, municipal offices of cement block; and on another, a chapel. There was nothing on the fourth side; a ravine lay below. Its municipal office was austere. Its only furnishings were, in the center of the room, a wide, unfinished pine table and bench, and in one corner, a second bench and file cabinet.

We talked with a man sitting behind the table. He was the president of the committee of the village properties, a slim, round-faced man who listened attentively as we spoke about the similarities among the various villages that, like this one, had contracts with the paper company. After speaking to him, we made our rounds in the village, handing out the leaflets and talking to people as we could. About two o'clock in the afternoon, we were ready to go back to Oaxaca.

We crossed the river and went back down the trail where we'd been frightened the night before, then waited by the side of the road for a bus to come. A pickup came our way and we stuck our thumbs out, asking for a ride. The pickup stopped. On its door was a sign saying that it belonged to the paper company. The driver was a middle-aged man with eyes as round as coins and short black hair that grew as perpendicular to his head as the quills on a porcupine.

"Where are you headed?" he asked.

"To Oaxaca City," I told him.

"I'm not going that far, but jump in anyway."

He made room for us in the cabin between boxes of tools that covered almost the whole floor. To make things more comfortable, he had me put my bag in the back of the pickup.

He said that he was a mechanic for the paper company. He said that the paper company sent him all over the region, and that he always gave rides to people. "The pickup isn't mine," he explained. "I don't pay for the gasoline, so why shouldn't I pick up people, as long as they're going the same way as me? I help them, because I don't charge what the bus companies do, and that way, I earn a little extra, at least enough to buy some beers."

He smiled a little smile.

A few kilometers later some *campesinos* came out from one of the little houses that break the vegetation at roadside. They stuck out their thumbs, and the driver stopped for them, too. They crawled into the back of the pickup, taking their belongings with them.

Before long we rounded a curve and came upon an intersection that was blocked by soldiers. Two military trucks were parked there, and soldiers were scattered up and down the roadside, their guns held at their chests. Another group of soldiers searched the vehicles that stopped. In front of us was a car with its trunk open. A soldier was taking suitcases out of the trunk.

"A roadblock," the driver said, making a gesture that showed that he felt it was a waste of time. "From time to time they're here, part of something called the Condor Plan, or so the newspapers say. They're looking for drugs."

I felt fear in the pit of my stomach. I inhaled deeply, exhaling with an open mouth, quietly. I took Magdalena's hand. She didn't seem nervous.

I didn't have any guns with me, but in the bag were leaflets and books. I was sure that they'd ask questions about them—and just how far they'd question me, I didn't know. I thought about what they might do to Magdalena.

The soldiers went to the back of our pickup. The *campesinos* were showing them what they carried. An officer came up to the window of the pickup, telling the driver to step out. He did. His movement gave me a couple of moments alone with Magdalena.

"Don't come with me," I whispered. "Tell them that you're with the driver."

Then I glanced at her; she understood my plan.

One by one, the *campesinos* pulled their bags to the edge of the pickup's bed. Their biggest bags contained coffee beans. Soldiers stuck their hands into the bags, feeling around inside. I watched as they searched the last *campesino*. My turn was coming up.

A soldier fixed his eyes on my bag.

"And what's in that bag?" he asked in a loud voice.

This is it, I said to myself. "Tools that I use on the job," I heard the driver say indifferently. "This guy and me work for the paper plant."

"You can go on," the officer told us.

I felt an immediate rush of gratitude towards the driver. His answer had come just in time.

~~~~~~~~~~~~

By the time that I had dropped Magdalena in Oaxaca City and returned to Tuxtepec, a movement courier had dropped off the newspapers. *El Comunero* was laid out just as we'd discussed: Zapata on one side of the top of its front page, Villa on the other. The issue carried a story about the lumber industry in the Juárez Mountains, and another about *cacique* rule in San Pedro Yolox. My friends and I decided that we'd take the papers into the mountains and find somebody to distribute them in each village. We'd charge our distributors two pesos for each copy, to cover our expenses.

My friends told me, that while I'd been on the road, Tío had moved from Miguel Hidalgo to a village closer to Tuxtepec. We decided to stop and see him on our way to the mountains. To get to his new quarters, we had to cross fields of pineapple and sugar cane, then go up a mountain. The *palapa* where he lived had been recently built, and consisted of three rooms: a bedroom, a kitchen, and a big room for receiving guests.

Besides Tío, Silvia, and the brown-haired girl, there was now another person there: a short, thin woman of about twenty-five with hair that fell to her shoulders. She was the wife of a *compañero* who was in jail in the state of Morelos.

Tío told us that, once again, he'd put off getting his ulcer treated until a better opportunity. He had other bad news, too. Valentín, the *compañero* who had been driving the tractor in Paso del Toro, was hospitalized in Mexico City. While returning from a visit to El Zacatal, he'd been ambushed. His escape had been almost miraculous. The first burst of gunfire had hit him in the legs and also lodged a bullet in one of his kidneys. He'd fallen to the ground, pulled out the .32 caliber pistol that he always carried, and begun crawling for a cornfield. He was only about four hundred meters from the village, and so, firing back at his assailants from time to time, he managed to keep them at bay. When the townsmen heard shots, our *compañeros* grabbed their rifles, and as they ran to where Valentín lay, they fired into the air. Their shooting scared the *pistoleros* away.

His wounds needed a doctor's attention, so they carried him to a hospital in Tuxtepec. But the hospital could not care for him, and sent him on to the General Hospital in Mexico City. When the police came to question him there, he told them that as far as he knew, the shooting was the result of a case of mistaken identity.

Before we left his side, Tío told us that he thought that we should spend the next four months building up the circulation of *El Comunero*. By giving vendors half of its cover price, we managed to get it displayed in news stalls in Oaxaca City. In the villages, a lot of people paid more than its two-peso price just to encourage its publication. The work was soon going well, but it was interrupted by another project.

———≈≈≈≈———

Drone had promised that we'd accompany the "floating population" to a general assembly in Yolox. The object of the plan, according to Melquíadez, who had thought it up, was to unmask the *caciques* in public, in front of the authorities, who would accompany us. Two representatives of the Agrarian Reform Ministry, an agent of the federal police, and a platoon of ordinary police officers were to be on hand. To take the "floating population" home, Melquíadez had rented a passenger bus, just like those that run from Oaxaca City to Tuxtepec.

On the appointed day, twenty-five of us got onto the bus, including the two representatives of Agrarian Reform. The federal and local police never arrived.

The two functionaries appeared to be just ordinary bureaucrats, the type who spend their days behind desks. They would have preferred to stay in the city, I'm sure, but some superior official must have ordered them into the field. Their shoes were shined but, had they stood up, they'd have had to stretch their necks to see them over their pot bellies. They spoke only to Melquíadez, who referred to them as *licenciados*.

Just like them, Melquíadez carried a briefcase. Inside were all of his documents, proofs of his legal filings before various agencies. He had drawn up an agenda for the meeting. Its principal demand was that the community be told what had become of the money that the paper company paid in royalties for timber rights. Another demand was that the *caciques* return to the community some plots of land that they'd commandeered. A third was the clarification of the murder charges for which Nemesio and Rosendo had been imprisoned.

It was about eleven in the morning when the bus pulled into Yolox. Noticing that a lot of people were hanging around, Melquíadez said, "They are waiting for us." The "floating population" got off the bus and headed towards the meeting hall, about a hundred meters away. By ones and twos, some of the people who were lolling about the streets formed a group around the newcomers, and when the group got to number about a dozen, its members began insulting the "floating population" in both Chinantec and Spanish. Melquíadez had already instructed the group not to say a word in answer. Everything that was to be said was to be spoken inside.

The meeting hall was about ten by fifteen meters in size, with a raised platform at its front. A big table and a long bench sat on the platform. Melquíadez and the two bureaucrats sat down there, alongside a man who said that he was the mayor. Benches of unpainted pine stood in rows facing the platform. A good number of *campesinos* came in, poorly dressed men in black tennis shoes or sandals; some of the sandals were those that have sections of automobile tires as soles. They didn't say much, confining themselves to twisting on the benches to look at one another, like schoolboys under the strict vigilance of a teacher. A couple of those in the group were better-fed and better-dressed than the others. The son of one of the *caciques* was on hand, standing in a corner near the platform. His eyes shot back and forth over the scene, as if he were watching for something to happen. The "floating population" stood in an aisle on one side of the meeting room.

When the assembly began, everyone became quiet. One of the *licenciados* began explaining the details of the law that authorized his presence. His only mission, he said, was to see that peace and tranquillity returned to the village.

Melquíadez spoke next. Slowly, measuring every word, he explained that the affairs of the village weren't as the *caciques* claimed, and that he and his people were struggling for the common good. Then he read his agenda and called for discussion of its first point.

We expected to hear a cascade of shouts, or maybe some applause. But nothing happened. Everything remained silent. The peasants sitting on the benches looked at one another, but they didn't speak.

It was the *cacique's* son who broke the silence. "How can it be that people of your rank," he asked the bureaucrats, "have let yourselves be deceived? These people left the community because they wanted to divide it rather than letting it work in harmony."

Then he turned to the audience and said, "It's really like that, isn't it, *paisanos*?"

Their reply came in unison: "Y-e-e-e-s."

Then he said that the villagers didn't need any clarifications when everything was already clear to them. It wasn't acceptable, he said, for a tiny group of undesirables to demand explanations from anybody.

"Isn't that the way that it is, *paisanos*?" he said to the throng.

"Y-e-e-e-s!"

Melquíadez and Nemesio spoke again, the latter saying that it wasn't right for him and his brother to have gone to prison for a murder that *pistoleros* hired by the *caciques* had committed. Then he gave names and dates.

"That's pure lies!" the son of the *cacique* said. "Isn't it a lie, *paisanos*?"

"Y-e-e-e-s!"

Speakers made other attempts to start a discussion, but only with the same results. Then one of the bureaucrats said that, in view of the assembly's failure to cooperate, other means would have to be sought. The meeting broke up.

A crowd was waiting at the exit, many of whose members hadn't been inside during the discussion. As the members of the "floating population" filed out, the crowd hurled insults at them again. Outside, another group was gathered, too—a group of people loyal to the *caciques*. Not more than a meter separated the two groups when someone in the "floating population" answered an insult by calling the townspeople "sell-outs" and "cowards." The scene immediately became a Babylon of invectives, and of course, somebody threw a blow. A free-for-all started: kicks, shoves, and punches. The people in the two groups looked like worms crawling on a piece of rotting meat. Three people were beating on Rosendo. Drone went to help him, but they threw him off, warning him, "Keep out of this, idiot!"

It seemed impossible for the "floating population" to come out ahead where the *caciques* were in charge, so I decided to turn to the only weapon at hand.

"Why don't you stop this?" I said to the Agrarian Reform bureaucrat who was nearest me. "You've got authority. People will obey you!"

His mouth dropped open and he looked at me with incredulity. How could I think that he could stop the brawl?

"They will obey you," I repeated.

For a few seconds he stared at the crowd, as if measuring his strength. Then he inflated his chest and with a firm step walked towards the fight.

"SEÑORES!" he shouted, raising his arms into the air. His briefcase was still in his right hand.

The blows stopped, the shouting ceased, and the two groups formed again, almost as if nothing had happened. Several members of the "floating population," unconscious or bleeding, remained on the ground. The bureaucrat, without saying anything more, simply shook his head, as if he were deeply disappointed.

If he had wanted to, I think the bureaucrat could have circulated a petition, and everybody present, on both sides, would have ratified his fitness for office.

The local group scattered into the streets again. The "floating population" got back onto its bus, carrying its wounded. Their crusade to reform San Pedro Yolox ended at the Red Cross clinic in Oaxaca City.

Our newspaper didn't miss an issue, though it was sometimes delayed. Each of us who took it into the rural areas returned with news to print in a subsequent issue. One of the towns that we visited was Natividad, a mining village about an hour and a half outside of Oaxaca City. Natividad looked like a ghost town. No children ran up and down its streets, and the adults who were sometimes seen crossing were always silent. If it hadn't been for smoke from the chimneys of its houses, one might have thought it deserted.

The decline of Natividad had begun when someone discovered that it had gold and silver beneath its soil. The deposits were in communal lands, but over the years, those riches had brought more misery than prosperity to the town. One of the products of its wealth was a man of about fifty-five who was sitting in an old chair at the edge of a room in his house, both hands resting on a cane. He sat without moving and his breathing was labored, as if he were eternally fatigued. His eyes bulged as if he were constantly curious, and his belly protruded like a big globe over his skinny legs. He was a disabled worker from the village mine. He'd been a miner all of his life, until dropsy struck him. The mine had paid him a miserly compensation, and his children had left town for the city, hoping for a better end for their own lives. His wife had died, as was evident: The walls of his two-room adobe house were bare, and its patio was devoid of flowers or other plants. He slept in a corner of the nearly derelict kitchen.

Between gasps, he told us that the town's miners had once been affiliated with the National Union of Mine, Metallurgical, and Kindred Workers, but some of the its leaders had been murdered, and the others bribed. The mine had wound up under the control of businessmen who had made the men work in the tunnels with only helmets for protection. The company opened up a store that gave credit to the miners, but as in Yolox, the workers always ended each week more in debt that when they'd begun.

There was a clinic in town, he told us, but nurses and doctors were rarely there. Some of the miners had come down with silicosis, and others were tubercular. When the miners came up from the tunnels, they were strip-searched for contraband wealth. Nobody had paid attention to what the air might do to their health. The situation in the village was hopeless. It reminded me of the truth of what Don Carlitos had said: "They only want what we have."

—〰〰〰〰—

On one of our trips to see Tío, sometime in early October, 1978, Tío asked how much support there might be in the Juárez Mountains for a land takeover in the Tuxtepec region. We told him that our Association didn't have enough strength to lend decisive aid, that about all that we could do was make sure that somebody put up signs along the highway, expressing solidarity.

"In that case, be ready for some news," he said.

Not long after we visited Natividad, Circus Man came back to Tuxtepec from a visit with Tío. He said the takeover would come the next day. On his trip he had witnessed the preparations. *Campesinos* from several areas were coming and going to and from Tío's hut; he didn't even have time to sit down to eat.

"Tío said for us not to let him down," Circus Man declared.

We got busy. Drone, Circus Man, and Beodo decided to skip their classes in Tuxtepec. All of us went to the village. Beodo got the cloth and paint for making banners. Circus Man helped letter them. Drone and I went to the city hall. I let him talk because I knew him to be a convincing speaker: We wanted the mayor to grant us permission to post the banners on village-controlled land next to the highway.

At first, the mayor and his assistants were hesitant, but Drone won them over. Then we went from door to door, talking to the people who we knew were sympathetic to the Association. We asked them to show their support in a town hall meeting, in case somebody questioned the mayor's decision. We did the same thing in a neighboring village.

We knew that a land takeover wasn't an affair that lasted only a day, and, therefore, we planned to post our banners gradually, so that it would look like support for the takeover was growing as the days went by. A day or two after we began, a copy of the Mexico City daily *Excelsior* came into our hands. "100,000 Indigenes Take Over

Properties in Oaxaca," its headline said. The article reported that, "In order to reclaim 150 thousand hectares of communal properties that were taken away by big planters, some one hundred thousand indigenes of the Valle Nacional, the Juárez Mountains and Jacatepec regions have begun invading the lands as part of a peaceful movement that threatens to extend across the state."

The article mentioned that the peasants involved had received a delegate from the Ministry of Agrarian Reform, who characterized the situation as "serious." The story, by a reporter whose job was to cover some one hundred and fifty villages, also included an interview with *compañero* Raúl: "We have decided to reclaim what the landlords have taken away," he said. "This isn't an 'invasion,' because we're just taking back what's ours."

My *compañeros* decided that I should visit the region where the action was. A few kilometers after my bus passed Valle Nacional, I got off, after seeing the first sign, one that said: "Mr. President, we pledge to you our unconditional support in getting rid of the big ranches and plantations once and for all." Not far ahead was the first contingent of peasants, who had installed themselves in a pasture so big that it would have taken a half-hour to walk the length of it. Off in the distance, so far away that it looked like a toy, was a tractor, plowing. It was turning under the pasture land. The *campesinos* would soon plant corn or beans or *chiles*—whatever *they* decided. They had taken a shed that had been used to water cattle and turned it into a meeting hall and kitchen. Driver was in charge of their group. They had divided into shifts that kept watch in turn, twenty-four hours a day. There was a spirit of camaraderie among the men.

"How do you like this little piece of land?" Driver said, turning his head from one horizon to the other. "Six months from now, we'll be able to invite you to eat corn, fried or grilled!"

Meanwhile we watched a carload of policemen pass down the highway.

"How is it going?" I asked.

"Well, a delegate from Agrarian Reform came by to scold us," he commented. "He told us to put our attitude aside, that we shouldn't be taking the law into our own hands. We told him that we were taking the law into our hands because the law itself had never done anything. He said, over and over again, that we'd better get off the land to avoid confrontations with its owners. 'But we're the owners!' a bunch of the guys told him. The delegate went on with a string of words that we didn't really understand, but what we did understand is that he was accusing us of a serious crime. The good thing about it is that Ernesto is here, a guy whose brain makes up for what his body lacks. He put the delegate in his place, shut his mouth as easy as taking a bite out of a taco. Ernesto asked him, 'Mr. Delegate, is Article 27 of the Constitution still in effect?' The delegate said that it was. 'And Section Six?' The delegate told him 'yes' again. 'And Section Eight?' For the third time, the delegate said yes. 'Then we're not committing any crime,' Ernesto said. 'We are strictly in compliance with what the Constitution sets forth.'

"Well, after that, the delegate said other things, but what I remember is that he said he'd go to Oaxaca City to inform the governor about what was happening, and that he'd come back after he'd been there."

The following day, I headed back to the village. As the bus rounded a curve near the place where our dirt road begins, I saw the acronym of the Association painted on the trunks of several trees and banners hanging between some of them. My *compañeros* had done their work as planned. They asked me about Tío's health, but nobody, I told them, had seemed to know exactly where he was.

A few days later we received a report that several trucks carrying soldiers had been seen on the highway, headed towards Valle Nacional, and afterwards we learned that the peasants had peacefully surrendered the land that they'd taken. They'd given the land back for two reasons. First of all, the delegate from the Ministry of Agrarian Reform had come back saying that he had instructions from President José López Portillo to personally resolve the conflict by the December 12, the feast day of the Virgin of Guadalupe. The second reason had been a threat. The captain in charge of the troops who stood on the highway had told the peasants that, "If you're not out of here by five o'clock in the morning, we're going to screw you somthing awful."

Tío accepted the surrender, although he knew that the government's promises couldn't be trusted. "We weren't ready, we weren't prepared," he told me later.

In the days following the surrender, platoons of policemen installed themselves at every highway intersection and at every place where dirt roads met on their way to villages that had participated in the takeover. A knot of *pistoleros* stood with every group of cops and soldiers. Their job was to identify the *compañeros*.

The Tuxtepec jail filled with *campesinos*. One of them was Raúl, the president and founder of the Association. His wife was the only person allowed to speak to him in jail. She told us that his wrists were inflamed from where they'd handcuffed him during torture. There were bruises all over his body. His eyes were infected, he was having difficulty breathing, and he complained of pain in his chest. During his interrogation, they'd hung him from his heels and beat on the soft parts of his body with a piece of wood. They'd also forced carbonated drinks down his nose. The policemen said that they wanted information about eleven killings in the region, but that, of course, was just a pretext: What they really wanted to know was who was behind the Association.

The authorities learned that Güero Medrano was in the region, and increased the number of men at their roadblocks. This attracted the attention of *Excelsior's* reporter. The new operation, a police commander told him, was aimed at capturing "Güero Medrano and his fifteen highwaymen." The harassment was so intense that the *campesinos* began to fear having Tío in the villages, let alone in their own homes. They didn't turn their backs on him, but Güero had to spend several days in an isolated shack in the mountains. Silvia and the little girl stayed below, at a secret location.

A few days earlier, Güero had almost fallen into the dragnet. He'd been returning with some of the locals from a day of labor in the fields of a village near Valle Nacional. Up ahead of them about three hundred meters, they'd seen a platoon of policemen. Tío had told his group to form a phalanx so that he wouldn't be seen as they walked through the roadblock. At the appropriate moment, he said, he'd disappear into the growth. The *campesinos* did as he told them, and he escaped unseen into the countryside.

Maybe it was because he was hiding in the woods and was eating irregularly, but Tío's ulcer began to act up during that time. He couldn't keep his food down, and he had a constant headache and a ferocious fever. He spent his time lying down.

"I was scared to death," he told us. "I believed that I was going to die in a pointless way, sick and alone in the middle of the mountains. Because I was feverish, I also imagined that the troops were coming, to catch me as easily as a bird already in a cage."

But the *campesinos* didn't leave him alone. They took food to him every day, and when they noticed that he was ill, they brought the village *curandera* as well. She made him drink hot cinnamon tea and swallow a couple of pills. Then she gave him a rubdown with alcohol and ordered him to lie down, covering himself from head to toe with blankets. Two hours later, Tío was sweating through his clothes.

A second treatment wasn't necessary. He was recuperating. The *campesinos* brought him milk and mild food that wouldn't inflame his ulcer.

I ran into him about a month later. The *compañeros* had found a safe hiding place for him in a hut of ordinary size on a little farm where only one family lived, in the area between Tuxtepec and Valle Nacional. The place wasn't more than three hundred meters from the federal highway, but to get there you had to walk up an incline so steep that your body seemed to almost hang off the mountainside.

Four people lived there: a peasant in his forties, his wife, a son in his twenties, and the grandfather, a gray-haired man who walked with a cane. The old man was a musician. He had made his four-string guitar himself, back in his adolescence. It was crude-hewn instrument, dark with age, dirt, and use. The old man tuned it to his own liking; when he strummed the chords, a muffled sound came out, as if the strings refused to sing. But the old man sang melodies that sounded as if they were to a *jarocho* rhythm, and even a professional would have envied the way he slapped the guitar box.

The family grew corn, and around their hut they had coffee plants. One plot of land they reserved for vegetables that they sold in the towns. I spent Christmas there, along with some *campesinos* from the nearby villages. New Year's Day found me still there, as, at the strike of midnight, those who had guns fired into the air to celebrate.

Tío and the local *campesinos* no longer talked much. The *campesinos* were probably discouraged because neither the president of Mexico nor anybody else had appeared to hand over titles to their lands on December 12. They had learned from bitter experience what things are like when one puts trust in the government.

"*Compañeros,*" Tío said to a group that had come to visit, "you have demanded that they give you back your lands legally, and they ignored you. You took over the lands, just to put pressure on them. They've responded with treachery and repression. You should learn that you're dealing with an enemy who is not going to give you back what's yours unless you take it for yourselves. Rich people don't understand anything that isn't said with guns."

A few days later Tío and I went to Oaxaca City. When we got there, he saluted me in a military fashion. "Tianguis, I'm your soldier. You tell me how I can help you in the mountains."

He explained that he needed to move. He said that they had two or three times seen cars with smoked windows pass slowly by on the highway below the little house on the mountainside. I went to see my *paisanos* in Tuxtepec, and we decided that the best place to hide him was in Circus Man's house. One dawn a pickup driven by a fat middle-aged man with a mustache like Cantínflas' drove Tío, Silvia, and the little girl into the village. They brought with them a cardboard box, half-filled with clothing, a couple of blankets, and a few kitchen utensils. That was all they owned.

I imagined for a minute that for the rest of my life I might see Tío here and there: In every village there were *compañeros* who would build or give him a house, and he could have spent his life in such retirement. But he wasn't a person who wanted to settle down or accumulate things. I asked myself how much one had to suffer or what one had to understand before giving up a peaceful, routine life, as he had done. But no answer came, and I knew that if I asked him, he'd say, "The goal is to make the Revolution." I'd heard him say that before, but for me, it wasn't a sufficient explanation.

To ready Circus Man's house for Tío's stay, all we had to do was come up with a couple of cots. But there wasn't much for him to do there. Don Carlitos and other people who liked our newspaper came by to chat with him, but their talks never ended in any plan of action. Then Rosendo and Nemesio came. After talking to them, Tío said that he wanted to give the problems of the Chinantecs a closer look.

The Association now had three or four members in that region. One was a twenty-five-year-old named Antonio, from the village of Totomoxtla. Through him we found a place for Güero and his family. As it turned out, Totomoxtla was where Magdalena was teaching. She saw to it that the brown-haired girl was enrolled in school.

Just like in the other towns, it wasn't long before a stream of peasants began arriving for chats at Güero's house in Totomoxtla. Güero even learned a few words of Chinantec, so that he could greet people in the local language.

One afternoon a representative of the local *campesinos* asked him, "How much money do you want for getting rid of the *caciques*?" Tío told him that he wasn't a *pistolero*. "If you hire some gunslinger," he said, "you'll just fall prey to some other parasite. You've got to learn how and why to organize." But at the same time, he promised that he'd do what he could to support any action that they took. I began to wonder if Old Man Matías' scenario was going to play out again.

Little by little, the members of the "floating population" got to know Güero, coming to town one or two at a time. The only one who wasn't informed was Melquíadez.

Meanwhile, Tío's relationship with the people from the Tuxtepec area grew more distant. Valentín, who had for a long time been his *compañero,* had recovered from his wounds and returned to Paso del Toro, but hadn't gotten in touch with Tío, maybe because of all of his moving around. The people who had come in city dress also didn't visit now, and Ernesto was late in arriving again.

To maintain contact, Tío sent me to visit the villages in the Tuxtepec region, to ask how things were going and to bring back a report. Everywhere I went, people asked about his health and sent their greetings. But the land question had been at a standstill since the December surrender. In Miguel Hidalgo, things were no worse, but not much better, either. Old Man Matías told me, "Tell the son-of-a-bitch to come visit us. We'll always make room for him, like one of our own." In El Zacatal I learned that *compañero* Raúl was still in jail. That was the last town that I visited before heading back towards the mountains.

As I walked towards the highway to catch a bus, I ran into a federal patrol. I was only a hundred meters away when I saw them; there was no chance to turn back. Despite the suffocating heat of the region, I felt a chill in my toes and feet. It went climbing up to my knees, to my stomach, to my arms, into my face and even, I believe, to the roots of my hair. But I kept walking.

It looked to me like the soldiers had a clear range of view for at least two hundred meters. There was no chance of running, and besides, I was limping from a bruise on my foot and a boil in my groin. The *curandera* in my village had told me to take a corn stalk and to massage the sole of my foot with it. I'd done that, but it hadn't helped.

As I got nearer to the soldiers, I exaggerated my limp, hoping to appear as harmless as possible. A military truck was parked on the trail and a half-dozen soldiers were standing around it.

I passed the first one.

"Good afternoon," I said, but the soldier acted as if he hadn't heard me.

As I was getting near the second soldier I had addressed, I noticed that his lips were moving.

"Stop right there," I heard someone say.

I stopped. Another soldier, who seemed to be in command, came from the other side of the truck. He asked me my name and I told him.

"Where are you coming from?"

"From El Zacatal," I said.

"Do you live there?"

"No."

"So what are you doing around here?"

"I came to look for the schoolteacher," I said. "But he's not here. I came to see if he would loan me some money."

"What's the teacher's name?" he asked me suspiciously.

I knew the first name of the teacher, but I didn't know the last name, and that made the officer more suspicious. He made me show him the sole of one of my shoes, and he looked it over carefully, as if he was looking for a pattern or a track. He also asked me where I was from, and why I wanted to borrow money from the teacher.

"I have a boil on my groin and I need to go see a doctor," I told him.

"Doctor, come over here for a minute!" the officer said without taking his eyes off me.

A soldier came over. I wasn't sure if he was a doctor or not. He wore a military uniform and his insignia didn't seem to be different from those of the other soldiers. He made me show him the wound and the boil.

"They're going to have to cut off your dick," he said with a diagnostic air. Everybody laughed but me.

Then the officer took me over to the back of the truck. He stuck his hand into a box and when he pulled it out, he had between his fingers a bunch of plants no more than ten centimeters long.

"What is this?" he asked, shoving the bunch towards my face.

I imagined that it was marijuana but I wasn't lying when I said that I didn't know. I'd never seen young marijuana plants.

"So you don't remember the teacher's last name?" he said.

"It's not that I don't remember, sir," I told him. "I've never asked. I've just known him by his first name."

The officer ordered me to get into the back of the truck. The other soldiers got in too. The truck headed towards the village.

When we got to the middle of El Zacatal, the officer leaned out the window of the cab and told a little boy to look for the chief of police. Five minutes later, somebody introduced himself to the officer. The soldiers took me down from the truck.

The chief of police was Eusebio, a thin, light-skinned man of about twenty-five.

"Put this guy in jail," the officer said, pointing to me. "Tomorrow we'll come back for him. And be careful not to let him escape. You've got to be responsible for him."

That said, the officer got back in the truck, which left for the highway.

Eusebio looked around, and then spoke to me.

"*Compañero*," he drawled, rubbing his forehead, "what a problem you've got us in. I can't put you in jail because we're both *compañeros* of Güero, and I can't let you go because the army will screw me. This is a serious problem."

About a dozen *campesinos* gathered in the street with us and Eusebio explained the situation to them. I needed to sit down because the boil was bothering me. I walked about ten meters away, sat down on a curb and lit a cigarette. Eusebio and the *campesinos* were deliberating and I let them talk. After awhile, Eusebio approached me.

"Like I told you, *compañero*," he said, "we're not going to lock you up. You'll stay in my house tonight. But I've got to ask you a very big favor: Don't escape. When night comes and the rest of the *compañeros* come in, we'll figure out what to do."

Eusebio lived on the edge of town. His wife and two daughters, three and five, were at home. They gave me something to eat and found a cot for me.

That night there was a meeting of El Zacatal's *compañeros*. When Eusebio came back, he told me what they'd decided. The next day they would keep an eye open, and when they saw the soldiers coming into town, they'd stop them and tell them that I had gotten sick and that Eusebio had taken me to a doctor. Meanwhile, Eusebio and I would be not far away, watching to see what developed.

They figured that the ruse would work because the soldiers hadn't come into the area looking for Güero's troops. They'd come because a car with blood on its seats had been found abandoned beside the highway. They might never come back to town, everybody seemed to think.

When Eusebio and his family retired for the night, I tried to sleep, but I couldn't. I kept wondering what to do the next day. It seemed to me that the officer might want to tie up loose ends, and if he was smart, he might be suspicious. After all, Raúl, the Association's director, who was in jail, was from El Zacatal. They knew that I didn't know the teacher's last name, and I'd been able to come up with a story explaining how I knew him, without mentioning the Association. But if they questioned him, the story that he would give might be different.

I was worried that the soldiers would ask me where Güero was. That was the problem. How many blows could I take before confessing? Turning it over in my mind, I recalled that Eusebio had said that he and I would be watching at a distance. Everything depended on how great that distance would be. I was asking myself if I was capable of knocking Eusebio over the head so that I could make my escape into the brush. The growth on the north side of the village was thick, and they'd never find me there.

When the sun came up my eyes felt swollen from lack of sleep and I ate breakfast without hunger. Eusebio left the house. He came back about eleven o'clock, nearly out of breath.

"They're coming. Let's go!" he panted.

In the middle of El Zacatal was a big *palapa* that was used as a meeting hall—the same place where, unknown to the soldiers, we'd held the congress. A big group of *compañeros* were there, gathered around a pickup that belonged to the state police. It hadn't been the soldiers who had come back, it was the state police. The cops were chatting with the *campesinos*.

"We'll wait here," Eusebio said when we came in sight.

I looked to one side. The woods were about a hundred and fifty meters away. My stomach grew tight and my mouth went dry. I lifted my bruised foot and bent my knee, to determine that yes, I could put up with the pain: Fear is a good anesthetic.

Then I looked over at Eusebio. He seemed nervous and he kept his eyes fixed on the police. If I saw that the police were coming towards us, I decided, I'd break for the woods. I studied Eusebio's physique. He was a few centimeters taller than me, and his arms were muscled. I wouldn't be able to knock him down with a single blow. But all I needed was to gain fifteen meters on him. He was wearing sandals. I had boots, in good condition. That was an advantage.

"What will Güero say about this?" I asked him, without expecting an answer, or wanting one. The night before I had asked and answered that question for myself in too many ways.

"They're leaving!" Eusebio exclaimed all of a sudden, making a broad gesture with his hands and arms.

Then after a minute, he added, "I need a good drink to put this behind us."

I was only too happy to toast. We went over to the group of *compañeros*, who told us that the state police hadn't really understood why the soldiers had told them to come to El Zacatal; they hadn't shown much interest in the story about Eusebio and me and that they didn't seem to plan on coming back anytime soon. Somebody went to buy a bottle. After we passed it around and I'd had a half-glassful myself, I was on my way back to Totomoxtla and Güero's house.

"Tianguis," Tío's daughter told me after coming home from school one morning that February, "the teacher put my name on the board with the names of the other girls. And do you know what? The other children came up and put a lot of marks after my name."

Magdalena brought Luchita—for that was the girl's name—home from Totomoxtla's school every day. The children had been voting, she explained to me. The school was going to have a festival to celebrate the coming of spring, and the children had elected Luchita as class queen. On the March 21, the school was decorated with paper flowers and crepe streamers, and a few natural flowers, too. They'd rigged up an assembly room at whose front hung a green curtain on which big cardboard letters had been pinned: "Luchita I, Queen of Spring."

For the event Luchita had been given a pink dress with lace and frills. Hanging from her shoulders was a long red velvet cape, which a little boy dressed as a page held at waist level, to keep it from touching ground. Silvia had gone to great lengths to find teardrop-shaped adornments for her hair.

After a brief ceremony at the schoolhouse, Luchita paraded down the main street of the village, waving at the inhabitants, who gathered at street side to applaud her. Then the children's parade returned to the school, where Luchita was seated between two chamberlains. The school's principal crowned her and gave her a scepter, declaring her queen. A festival more than an hour long followed, as other students performed regional dances.

"My Lord!" Tío said as he took Luchita in his arms after the cere-monies. "You're so little, and you're already a queen?"

A few days later, Tío grew tired of wondering where Ernesto was. He sent me to Mexico City to hunt for him again, and to find out, again, why the next issue of *El Comunero* was late in coming out.

That night, members of the "floating population" came into town. They'd gotten in around four in the morning and come directly to Tío's house. We sent them to stay at the homes of other *compañeros*. This time, it wasn't a big land seizure being planned. Only the members of the "floating population" would be involved, only in Yolox, and they would take over a small piece of land. They would put it into cultiva-tion immediately. They wouldn't wait for the intervention of the Agrarian Reform Ministry, I was told. Before I left for Mexico City, I watched Güero and the men from the "floating population" set off at a march. I wanted to go with them, but I wasn't from Yolox or even a Chinantec. Güero said that my work with the newspaper was, in the long run, as important as the coming action in Yolox.

As soon as I got to Mexico City the next day, I made a phone call from the bus station to my friend Benjamín, just to stay in touch. He had just talked to someone at home and had bad news for me. The news was alarming, though its details I wouldn't learn for months.

Federal troops had gone into Macuiltianguis about sunup and taken up positions throughout the town. They had a list of names. When the first of the *paisanos* left their houses, going to the fields, the troops had grabbed them and forced them to point out the houses where the suspects lived. They had gone to the homes of Beodo, Circus Man, Drone, and Magdalena.

Nobody was home at Beodo's place, but the soldiers found an old Mauser there. Drone had been warned as the soldiers approached town; by the time they rousted his family, he was gone to the woods. The troops had found Magdalena in her parent's house and had taken her to the town square, where they asked about Güero's whereabouts, slapping her repeatedly across the face. At first, she denied knowing him, but when they threatened to undress her in front of everyone, she'd had to tell them.

Then they started looking for my house, my parent's home. On one of the streets they ran into a young *paisano* who, as always, was headed to the communal pasture to check on his cattle. As always, he was carrying his .22 rifle with him. The soldiers disarmed him, then gave him a beating. When they got finished, they told him to show them where my family lived. He told them that he was a teacher who was only a visitor in town, that he made his home in the neighboring village. They repeated their questions, beating him all the while. He stuck with his story. While they were interrogating him, another *paisano* walked by; they persuaded him to lead them. They picked the hapless "teacher" up from the ground, told him that he was under arrest, and began pushing him along in front of them.

Everyone was asleep at my house, but a couple of good blows from a rifle butt opened the door to Benito's bedroom. They pulled him outdoors, still in his underwear, and turned his room upside down in a search that produced only a .22 rifle that we'd always had. Outside, they started beating him. Between their blows they asked, "Where is your brother?" "Where are the guns?" "Where is Güero Medrano?" On one side of the yard they had posted the *paisano* who'd said that he was a teacher. His upper lip was now swollen and covered with blood.

The troops didn't waste much time before breaking into my parent's bedroom, taking out my father, and questioning him in the same way. He instinctively raised his hands to stop a blow, and in doing so, knocked the eyeglasses from a torturer's face. For that, he got a double beating.

Octaviano, the *paisano* who had said that he was a teacher, must have noticed that his guards were momentarily distracted. He took off running, and he was fast. He was young and one of the better basketball players in town. He was nearly a hundred meters away before anybody knew that he'd gone. An officer yelled out a command that some of the troops chase him. They took off running, but lost sight of him. He had meanwhile gone into the door of a house, surprising its residents, who of course knew him well. He crawled under a table that had a long covering of oilcloth, trying to catch his breath. He and the residents heard the troops go by, asking people in loud voices if they'd seen anybody run down that street. The residents who were giving Octaviano refuge bolted their door, and pretty soon, the soldiers moved on down the street. They never recaptured him.

When the troops had finished questioning Benito and my father, they marched them down to the square. A *paisano,* seeing that Benito was wearing only his underwear, took off his jacket and ran behind the procession until he caught up. Then he tried to give the jacket to Benito. The soldiers stepped in his way and sent him off—without his jacket—swinging their rifle butts at him and shouting threats. After they got to the square, the soldiers let my father go. But they took Benito and Magdalena.

Circus Man had been the luckiest of our lot. He'd been home. His mother had gone out to gather firewood for the morning's cooking chores. She had seen the soldiers coming and had run back to warn her son. He bolted into the bushes, none too soon: He watched as they entered the house. But he wasn't staying put.

There was a trail between our village and Totomoxtla, where Güero was living. At a normal pace, the trip took three hours. That morning, Circus Man ran it in an hour and a half. When he got there, Tío wasn't home; he was in Yolox. But Silvia and Luchita were there. They gathered up a bag of belongings and set out for the highway to catch a bus for Oaxaca City, where they planned to hide. They were lucky. The bus came before the troops did. When the soldiers came into Totomoxtla and found Güero's house empty, they took reprisals, arresting the family's landlord and a couple of unlucky *campesinos.*

Silvia had told Circus Man where she planned to go. He went off towards Yolox to take word to Güero. On the trail, he ran into one of the members of the "floating population," who was going towards Totomoxtla, with news of his own. His mission, he said, was to inform Silvia that Güero had been seriously wounded.

The men who had come to take the land were composed of two groups. Most were refugees, but a few had come from Yolox. They had met up in a shack with thick wooden walls to establish a headquarters. They'd dispatched a man named Tiberio—a brother to Nemesio and Rosendo—to bring them firewood for cooking.

Tiberio had gone off into the woods. About this time Tío stepped out of the shack to take a look at the dawn. He heard a shot and Tiberio's scream, then felt a blow to his arm and chest. He threw himself to the ground, crawled into the hut, and ordered that everybody drop to the floor and take cover. Within seconds a deafening hail of bullets began striking the hut.

In the middle of the fusillade, Tío organized a defense. About a dozen of the men inside were armed, some with M-1 carbines, some with .22s, a few with pistols. Five men went out firing to their left, five more to their right. The unarmed men crawled out between the two lines. The assailants were in the woods; nobody could see them. But they stopped firing and when they did, Güero and a few others came out, shooting. They, too, ran for the woods. They were barely in the brush when they came upon Tiberio's body. He had two bullet wounds in his stomach and one in his head. The unarmed men picked up the body and the group moved on. Güero told them to split up, so as not to make a big target, and to keep moving until they were a good distance away from the scene. He, Rosendo, Nemesio and another *compañero* formed one group. Tiberio's father and the men carrying Tiberio's formed another.

A few hundred yards into the woods, Tío walked over to a tree, wrapped both arms around its trunk, and slid to the ground.

"I can't take it," he moaned to the others, his head bent to his chest.

Nemesio watched Tío open and close his eyes as if it he couldn't see well. He bent over to look at Tío's arm. The bullet had gone through his arm and into the right side of Tío's chest. The hole was perfectly shaped, and not much blood had oozed onto his shirt. Tío grabbed tightly onto the tree trunk, telling them that he couldn't keep walking. The brothers picked him up, and though they were shorter, took turns in helping him move further into the woods.

Finally they came to a settlement called Rancho Cerro Fruta. They asked for help and one of the residents offered his house and cot. Circus Man and the member of the "floating population" that he'd encountered on the trail reached Cerro Fruta several hours later. Güero was spitting blood and speaking only faintly by then.

Tío told him to go to the house of a *compañero* in a village near Valle Nacional. He dictated a telephone number. "Tell the *compañero* to go to Mexico City, dial the number, and say that I've got a wound in one lung," he instructed. After he'd delivered the telephone number, Circus Man was to return to the settlement and report that he'd made contact. Then he'd have to go back to the same village, Tío said, to wait for the messenger's return.

After learning of the arrest of my brother and Magdalena, I tried to figure out what to do. Standing there in the bus station, by pure chance I caught sight of a man I knew only as El Guicho. I'd seen him only once before, during the October land seizure. I told him what had happened in my village. He already knew about Tío's wound, and he told me of it. He was the messenger from the Valle Nacional village. He said that he was waiting for a man who would be carrying a doctor's bag, wearing a tan shirt and a light blue windbreaker. I decide to wait with him.

The doctor came on time. He was a young man with light skin and curly hair, a man I knew well: the elusive Ernesto. We boarded a bus for the village near Valle Nacional.

The federal troops had spread out across the mountains once they learned where Güero had been living. The men who had ambushed Güero got caught in the net. The troops drew their guns on them. One of them took off running into the woods. The troops fired, and he was wounded. The others were interrogated. They told the soldiers that they were *pistoleros* doing their duty. Instead of punishing them, the soldiers used them as guides to the mountains. They wanted them to help track down the guerrilla warrior or his corpse.

After he'd delivered the phone number to El Guicho, Circus Man had returned to the settlement, to Tío's side. Tío was vomiting blood, stammering in between spasms. He couldn't hold food down. He alone knew what kind of pains he was suffering, but he asked his keepers to hang him upside down for awhile, then return him to the cot.

He knew that he was dying. He asked Circus Man to take his watch and keep it for Luchita. Then he instructed Circus Man to give his pistol to Silvia when the time came. But for now, he said, he'd hang onto it, just in case the army found him. He picked it up from his bed and held it between his hands. He was holding it when he died.

The locals helped the militants of the "floating population" bury Tío in the settlement's little graveyard. Two days later the soldiers came. They forced the locals to dig up Güero's grave, and they took fingerprints of the body. Just to be sure, the locals said, soldiers cut off one of Tío's index fingers and took it with them.

Then the *campesinos* reburied Florencio Medrano Mederos, just as they'd reburied Francisco Villa and Emiliano Zapata before him. Another hero of the Mexican peasantry joined our history—and our hopes—in martyrdom.

～～～～～

The pickup moved slowly. It turned at a corner, then another. I more or less knew the neighborhood and tried to keep track of where we were. But it was useless. The pickup kept turning corners.

Rat Face straddled my brother's neck and from somewhere came up with a long, thin strip of cloth, which he used to blindfold him. He did the same to Fabían and then me. After that, everything was darkness.

Before long, the pickup entered what had to be an avenue, because the driver picked up speed and the sound of traffic was louder. Every now and then he would stop, probably for traffic lights. I heard the voices of pedestrians, and I thought of shouting that the police were kidnapping us. But it was just an idea: Nobody would have done anything for us. In Mexico City, everybody minds his own business. Besides that, since we were lying on the floor of the pickup, they couldn't have seen us and wouldn't have known where the shouting had come from. All I would have gotten for shouting would have been a couple of good blows from Toltec Head.

How the police got the address where my brother and Fabían were living, I don't know. But having heard of the assault on Macuiltianguis, the two had stayed in place, not suspecting that the cops would come to the apartment for them. The police had given them a few blows, until they were willing to turn over the names and addresses of my friends. That's how the trap had been set that I walked into like a lamb.

The pickup turned off the avenue and a few seconds later came to a halt. They made us crawl out, and with pushes and shouts they guided us down what was probably a hallway. From the light that came through our blindfolds, we knew that we were indoors.

We went up some stairs, then down another hallway, then up some more stairs, climbing in a spiral. The climb led us up to what had to be the roof of the building, because sunlight came through our blindfolds. I heard a metal door open and was pushed in. A blow to my chest threw me back against a wall, and a fist in my stomach nailed me there. I doubled over in pain. I could hear other doors opening.

The door in front of me slammed shut. I listened, trying to discern if I was now alone. No insult, no blows, no sound of footsteps; it seemed safe. Nevertheless I remained doubled over, not moving. A little later I heard steps going back down the stairs.

I was still blindfolded, and everything was dark. The door couldn't have bars, I figured, because if it did, some ray of light would have filtered in. I asked myself where they'd put Alfonso and Fabían, and I listened, hoping to hear some movement from them. But everything was quiet.

Slowly I stood up, still keeping my back to the wall. I took small steps to one side until I bumped into a corner, then walked forward until I did the same. The room was four paces on one side, two and a half on the other.

The floor was of concrete. I sat down. What else was there to do? Since the mind doesn't go blank, I found myself thinking, thinking about what would become of me. People I knew, such as *Compañero* Tomás, were in jail at Tuxtepec, and others were probably locked up elsewhere. I didn't think that the police would kill all of us, but it seemed likely to me that all of us wouldn't live, either. The problem was knowing which of us would die.

Hours later I heard hurried steps, those of at least two people. A door opened, I heard insults shouted, then a whine, then a cry and then the sound of somebody falling. The insults kept up, accompanied by the sounds of blows that, I suspected, were kicks. The moaning and crying continued.

I tried to recognize the sufferer's voice. It didn't seem to be that of either Fabián or my brother. It was the voice of somebody who didn't speak Spanish well. My palms started sweating, my stomach grew taut, and I could feel my heart beating as I realized that the same treatment was probably waiting for me. I felt frightened, depressed, and guilty at the same time—guilty because I felt responsible for the presence of Alfonso and Fabián in this place, and for the jailing of Magdalena and Benito as well. If I were questioned, I could speak for their innocence—but what good would it do?

I don't know if I fainted or eventually fell asleep, but I was awakened by somebody pulling my hair.

"Just look at the *hijo de la chingada*, sleeping like it was nothing," a voice said.

I raised my head, but it was still dark and I was still blindfolded.

"We know everything. You're only going to confirm it," the voice said in a threatening tone. "Who is going to take Güero's place?"

"I don't know," I said. It was true.

"Who is Pelos?"

"I don't know."

A couple of kicks hit me in the chest, knocking the wind out of me.

They waited a minute until I caught my breath and then asked me again. But the truth was, I didn't know any Pelos. So they kicked me again. This time I saw yellow flashes before my eyes.

"Leave him alone," the voice said. "We'll come back for him later."

The door closed again.

I tried to keep track of the passing days, but it was like keeping track of the corners we'd turned in the pickup. One loses track, loses one's bearings. I couldn't tell day from night, and sometimes, to further confuse my sense of time, I fell asleep.

Once, the door opened and somebody took off my handcuffs and put into my hands a sandwich and a cold drink in a paper carton. But I wasn't hungry, no matter how many days it had been. When I tried to eat the sandwich anyway, my teeth hurt. They felt like they were coming loose from the gums. After a while, the voice told me to put my hands behind my back again. I did, and the handcuffs were put back into place.

Shortly, I heard somebody screaming in pain. Was it Fabían? One of my brothers? Magdalena? I was comforted only when I judged that the voice wasn't female.

One day they dragged me out of the cell and took me to what seemed to be a yard. It was sunny and the warmth felt like a balm on my skin. I was told to stay standing where they'd put me, and I heard others being given the same order. Someone was pacing in front of us, striking the ground with some kind of stick or baton as he walked. Apparently, they had lined us up in file.

They hadn't brought us out for the sunshine, but to stand for hours, with orders not to speak or move.

"Quiet!" shouted a guard with a metallic voice.

One of us coughed and I could hear a blow.

"I said for you to stay quiet, mouths closed," the guard said.

It was nearly impossible to stay still. I kept wanting to shift my weight from one foot onto another. Somebody must have done that: I heard blows again.

The guard kept passing in front of us. I heard him hit others with his club as he went along. When he came to my place, I felt his fist on the tip of my nose, and then a push on my cheek, forcing me to turn my head sideways. I relaxed: Maybe he didn't mean to hit me, just to frighten me. He went past me, on down the line.

The sun had gone down and the warmth had gone away before they took us back to our cells. Exhausted, I lay on the floor. Different places on my body seemed to be pulsing, from bruises, maybe. It hurt to breathe. My muscles ached as if I had run a hundred kilometers.

A person can fall off to sleep in conditions like that, but at any minor movement or noise, one wakes up, afraid. The blood pulses in the temples, the seconds tick by, and the idea of death runs around in the brain. But that's senseless, too, and one figures out as much. Nothing matters except what *they* have planned, and one doesn't know what that is.

It soon became clear that the guards were following a routine. The sandwich and the cold drink in the paper carton were repeated, and the the marches to the yard, too. The long hours of standing—the slugs and blackjack blows—all of that happened again. The second time that we were standing in the yard, they started beating somebody about the time that the sun went down. They asked about guns. The man being tortured said that he didn't know where any guns were, didn't even know if there *were* guns. If we hadn't been blindfolded, from the noise we heard, we would have thought that the guards were fighting with somebody who was punching back. But the man didn't change his story, and after a while, they left him alone.

That day after we were returned to our cells, my turn came. The door of my cell opened, somebody grabbed me by the neck of my shirt and pulled me out to the yard, where they sat me down. A little ways off, I could hear them questioning somebody whose voice sounded like that of Fabián. They wanted to know what he knew about the movement. He told them about his daily routine and denied knowing anything about Güero's. They struck him. He repeated himself, and they struck him again. Perhaps to get them to let up, Fabián told them that one time he came home to the apartment and found us studying Marxism. Far from stopping them, it encouraged them.

"*Chinguenlo*, he knows more," a voice said.

The blows kept landing.

"Did you hear that?" a voice next to me asked.

"Fabián doesn't know anything and my brothers don't either," I said.

Kicks spun me around. Hands pulled on me until I was back in a seated position.

"What kind of weapon did you carry?" the voice asked.

"I didn't have a gun," I said.

The kicks came again.

"Where are the guns?"

"I don't know about any guns," I groaned.

"Don't play stupid. We know that you bought guns," the voice said before the kicks came again.

"One time I bought a gun," I gasped when I could, "but it was an old rusty Mauser that didn't have any cartridges."

"Who sold it to you?

"A *paisano*."

"His name."

"Anastasio Gómez," I told them, not worried, because the man had been dead for more than a year.

"You be careful with what you tell me," the voice warned, "because we're writing it all down and we're going to confirm it."

"When did you meet Güero Medrano?"

"I was a member of the Indigenous Association for *Campesino* Self-Defense," I began. I told them about the leaflet that we distributed, and about producing *El Comunero*. I told them that I'd met Güero at an Association meeting, that he'd given us advice on how to produce the paper.

"So what you're saying is that the son-of-a-bitch Güero Medrano took over the newspaper and the Association?"

"That's right," I told them.

The questioning stopped. I tensed myself for more kicks, but they didn't come.

Later on they pulled me to my feet and made me walk until they threw me into a room. It wasn't the same room as before, because next to me I felt another body. One of the bodies was speaking in a low voice, in a dialect that I didn't understand. The body next to me moaned, and the sound that I heard reminded me of Benito.

"Is it you?" I asked.

"Yeah, it's me."

"How are you doing?"

"Bad," he said. "If they beat me again, I don't think I'll make it."

I didn't say anything for a little while.

"Make yourself strong," I advised. But the phrase seemed hollow and false to me as soon as I said it. How can anyone make himself strong when completely defenseless?

I crawled over to where my brother lay, and, finding his body, placed an elbow over his arm, as if we were supporting one another, arm-in-arm, as in our boyhoods. Because he and I were the oldest of the family, the outdoor chores, such as bringing firewood and herding the cattle, had always fallen to us. Though my brother was a year ahead of me in school, he always looked out for me, and we had always joined to fight together in schoolyard quarrels. It was that feeling of solidarity that I hoped to rekindle on the floor of that cell.

A few hours later somebody came for me. My arms were still clasped with handcuffs behind my back. The guard unlocked them, had me put my hands together in front of me, then cuffed me again from the front. He marched me out of the cell and downstairs. A faint light entered the blindfold when we entered a room where I heard the sound of typing. They had me sit down in front of desk, where someone asked me to answer questions.

A few seconds later, they brought somebody else. As soon as I heard the answer to the first question, I recognized the voice. It was Magdalena. I was relieved at the tone of her voice: firm and sure, with her peculiar intonation. She had no difficulty in speaking. Maybe they hadn't tortured her, I thought.

The typing in front of me stopped. The guard put a pen between my hands, and guided them to a spot on a paper. I signed. They put another sheet of paper in front of me; I signed. Then another, and another. I couldn't see what I was signing, and I had no idea what it said. When the signing was over, they returned me to my cell.

Two or three days later they took us out to the yard again and seated us against a wall. We heard steps coming. They came to where we were and then stopped. A couple of seconds passed and then someone said that they were setting us free.

Three hours later, Fabián, Alfonso, and I were taken downstairs and put into the back seat of a car. Our handcuffs and blindfolds were removed. As the car passed through the streets going towards the apartment, I tried to look outside, but it was dark and the passing lights made me feel seasick. I bent my head down, trying to control the dizziness. A big man was riding in the front seat—a man so big that his shoulders rose above the backrest and his head touched the headliner. As we came into the neighborhood where the apartment was, he threw an arm over the backrest and looked at us.

"So, how many did you kill?" he asked, looking at me. His tone wasn't hostile. It was humorous.

"I haven't killed anybody," I said.

"We've been following Güero's trail for years," he said, almost nostalgically, as if commenting on a co-worker's retirement.

I didn't respond, and he said nothing more. The car stopped and we got out. Within seconds, we were free men again.

———≈≈≈∖∖∖———

Güero's movement was confused, inspiring, dangerous, tragic, but mainly woefully small and premature. It had led us to the terrifying scenes in jail, but rather than die there, dramatically, even heroically, as I'd imagined, I died—at least, a part of me did—in the back seat of that police car when the cop spoke those words. The bullet that wounded me wasn't made of copper or lead, but of routine. Our attempt to raise up our humbled people had been an important part of our lives. But for the political police, squashing it was just in a day's work.

About the Author

Ramón "Tianguis" Pérez is nicknamed for his birthplace, San Pablo Macuiltianguis, a Zapotec village in the Sierra Juárez region of Oaxaca, where his family ran a cabinet-making shop. While still in his teens, he became involved with the revolutionary movement of Florencio Medrano (known as "El Güero" or "Tío") in the *campo* of southern and central Mexico. After the collapse of Medrano's movement, Mr. Pérez survived by working variously as a carpenter, busman, laborer, printer, and furniture maker in both the United States and Mexico. His experiences as a *mojado* were chronicled in his first book, *Diary of an Undocumented Immigrant,* praised by *The Texas Observer* as "a remarkably honest first-person account that belongs to the rich tradition of Latin American testimonial literature and our own oral history . . . These are wonderful stories." Today Ramón Pérez and his wife, Mary, live in the state of Veracruz, where he works as a photographer.

About the Translator

Dick J. Reavis, a 1990 Nieman Fellow in Journalism, is a former newspaper reporter and senior editor of *Texas Monthly* who has written for numerous publications. Among his own books are *Conversations With Moctezuma: Ancient Shadows over Modern Life in Mexico* and *The Ashes of Waco: An Investigation,* a widely acclaimed study of the catastrophic 51-day siege of David Koresh's "Branch Davidian" movement by U. S. government agents. Today he divides his time between the Dallas area and Austin, where he is a senior editor for *Texas Parks and Wildlife* magazine. He first met Ramón "Tianguis" Pérez while reporting on guerrilla activities in Mexico, and subsequently translated Mr. Pérez's first book, *Diary of an Undocumented Immigrant.*